Microservices with Kubernetes

Non-Programmer's Handbook

Book 1: Microservices Architecture Handbook

Non-Programmer's Guide for Building Microservices

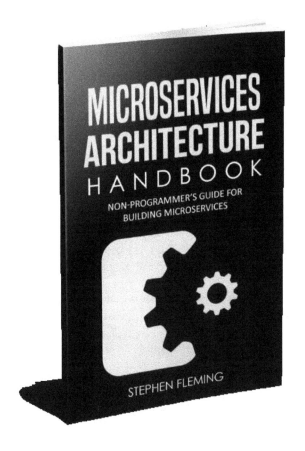

BONUS MICROSERVICES BOOKLET

Dear Friend,

I am privileged to have you onboard. You have shown faith in me and I would like to reciprocate it by offering the maximum value with an amazing gift. I have been researching on the topic and have an excellent "Microservices Booklet" for you to take your own expedition on the subject to next level.

- Do you want to know the best online courses to begin exploring the topic?
- Do you want to know major success stories of Microservices implementation?
- What are the latest trends and news?

Also, do you want once in a while updates on interesting implementation of latest Technology; especially those impacting lives of common people? "Get Instant Access to Free Booklet and Future Updates"

Type Link:
http://eepurl.com/ds8sfD

or

QR Code : You can download a QR code reader app on your mobile and open the link by scnning below:

1. Introduction

As the disruption of technologies continues to play a role in our lives, the application development process is becoming more flexible and agile. You must have heard about the concepts of Agile, DevOps, Kanban and many more. All these terminologies are basically making the application of development or the program writing exercise more flexible, more independent, and faster.

The Microservices architecture develops an application as a collection of loosely coupled services which is meant for different business requirements. Therefore, this architecture supports the continuous delivery/deployment of large, complex applications. It also enables the organization to evolve its application development capabilities.

Who can use this book?

This book can be used by a beginner, Technology Consultant, Business Consultant and Project Manager who are not directly into coding. The structure of the book is such that it answers the most asked questions about Microservices. It also covers the best and the latest case studies with benefits. Therefore, it is expected that after going through this book, you can discuss the topic with any stakeholder and take your agenda ahead as per your role. Additionally, if you are new to the industry, and looking for an application development job, this book will help you to prepare with all the relevant information and understanding of the topic.

2. Monolith and Microservices

Microservices

In May 2011, a workshop of software architects was held in Venice and coined the term "Microservices" to relate to an upcoming software architectural technique that many of the software architectures had been researching. It wasn't until May 2012that Microservices was approved to be the most appropriate term to describe a style of software development. The first case study relating to Microservices architecture was presented by James Lewis in March, 2012, at the 33rd Degree in Krakow in Microservices-Java the Unix way. To date, numerous presentations about Microservices have been made at various conferences worldwide, with software architects presenting different designs and software components of Microservices and its integration to different platforms and interfaces, such as Microsoft architecture and URI interface. Currently, Microservices has grown incredibly and has become an ideal way of developing small business applications, thanks to its efficiency and scalability. This software development technique is particularly perfect for developing software or applications compatible with a range of devices, both developed and yet to be developed, and platforms.

Microservices Defined

A standard definition of Microservices is not yet available, but it can be described as a technique of software application development which entails developing a single application as a suite of independently deployable, small, modular service. Every service controls processes and communicates with each other through a well-defined,

13

lightweight mechanism, often as HTTP resource API to serve a business goal. Microservices are built around business capabilities and are independently deployable by a fully automated deployment mechanism. They can be written in different programming languages such, as Java and C++ and employ different data storage technologies to be effective in the central management of enterprises or small businesses.

Microservices communicate to one other in several ways based on the requirements of the application employed in its development. Many developers use HTTP/REST with JSON or Protobuf for efficient communication. To choose the most suitable communication protocol, you must be a DevOps professional, and in most situations, REST (Representation State Transfer) communication protocol is preferred due to its lower complexity compared to other protocols.

Monolith Defined

A monolith is a software application whose modules cannot be executed independently. Thismakes monoliths difficult to use in distributed systems without specific frameworks or ad hoc solutions, such as Network Objects, RMI or CORBA. However, even these approaches still endure the general issues that affect monoliths, as discussed below.

Problems of Monoliths

1. Large-size monoliths are hard to maintain and evolve due to their complexity. Finding bugs requires long perusals through their code base.

2. Monoliths also suffer from the "dependency hell," in which adding or updating libraries results in inconsistent systems that either do not compile/run or, worse, misbehave.

3. Any change in one module of a monolith requires rebooting the whole application. For large projects, restarting usually entails considerable downtimes, hindering the development, testing, and maintenance of the project.

4. Deployment of monolithic applications is usually suboptimal due to conflicting requirements on the constituent models' resources: some can be memory-intensive, others computational-intensive and others require ad hoc components (e.g. SQL-based, rather than graph-based databases). When choosing a deployment environment, the developer must compromise with a one-size-fits-all configuration, which is either expensive or suboptimal with respect to the individual modules.

5. Monoliths limit scalability. The usual strategy for handling increments of inbound requests is to create new

instances of the same application and to split the load amongst said instances. Moreover, it could be the increased traffic stresses only a subset of the modules, making the allocation of the newer resources for the other components inconvenient.

6. Monoliths also represent a technology lock-in for developers, which are bound to use the same language and frameworks of the original application

7. The Microservices architectural style has been proposed to cope with such problems as discussed above.

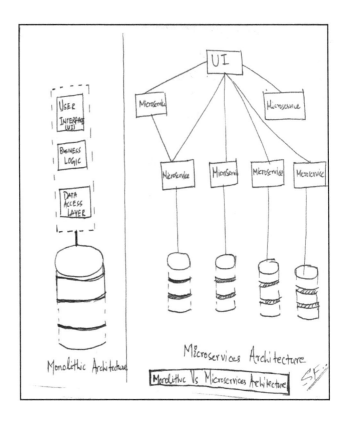

Future of Microservices

Over the years, software application development has evolved from Service-Oriented Architecture (SOA) to monolith architecture and now microservices architecture, which is the most preferred software application technique. Global organizations such as Amazon, eBay, Twitter, PayPal, The Guardian, and many others have not only migrated but also embraced microservices over SOA and Monolith architectures in developing their websites and applications. Will Microservices be the future of software application development? Time will tell.

Microservices compared to SOA

Microservices vs. SOA has generated lots of debate amongst software application developers, with some arguing that microservices is simply a refined improved version of SOA, while others consider microservices as a whole new concept in software application development which does not relate in any way with SOA. Nonetheless, microservices have a lot of similarities to SOA. The main difference between SOA and microservices may be thought to lie in the size and scope as suggested by the term "micro, "meaning small. Therefore, microservices are significantly smaller compared to SOA, and are deployed as an independent single unit. Furthermore, an SOA entails either numerous microservices or a single monolith. This debate can be concluded by referring to SOA as a relative of microservices. Nevertheless, they all perform the same role of software programme development, albeit in different ways.

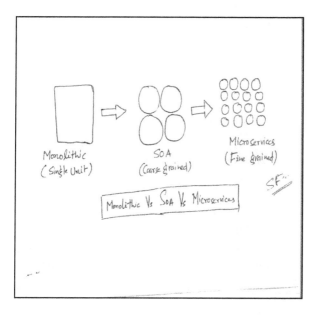

Monolithic (Single Unit) → SOA (Coarse grained) → Microservices (Fine grained)

Monolithic Vs SoA Vs Microservices

Features of Microservices Architecture

The features of microservices architecture differs widely as not all microservices have the same properties. However, we have managed to come up with several features that may be deemed appropriate and repetitive in almost all microservices.

Independent Deployment

Microservices are autonomous and can be deployed separately, making them less likely to cause system failures. This is done using components, which are defined as a unit of software that is independently replaceable and upgradeable. In addition to components, microservices architecture utilizes libraries or services. Libraries are components attached to a program using in-memory function calls. On the other hand, services are out-of-process components that communicate through different mechanisms, such as web service request mechanism Microservices applications. Software componentization involves breaking them into miniature components, termed as services. A good microservices architecture uses services as components rather than libraries, since they are independently deployable. An application consisting of multiple libraries cannot be deployed separately in a single process, since a single change to any component results in development and deployment of the entire application. An application consisting of multiple services is flexible and only a service is redeployed, rather than the entire application from a change in numerous service changes. It is therefore advantageous over library components.

Decentralized Data Management

This is a common feature in most Microsystems and involves the centralization of conceptual models and data storage decisions. This feature has been praised by small business enterprises, since a single database stores data from essentially all applications. Furthermore, each service manages its own database through a technique called Polyglot Persistence. Decentralization of data is also key in managing data updates in microservices systems. This guarantees consistency when updating multiple resources. Microservices architecture requires transactionless coordination between services to ensure consistency, since distributed transactions may be difficult to implement. Inconsistency in data decentralization is prevented through compensating operations. However, this may be difficult to manage. Nonetheless, inconsistency in data decentralization should be present for a business to respond effectively to real-time demand for their products or services. The cost of fixing inconsistencies is less compared to loss in a business experiencing great consistency in their data management systems.

Decentralized Governance

The microservices key feature is decentralized governance. The term governance means to control how people and solutions function to achieve organizational objectives. In SOA, governance guides the development of reusable service, developing and designing services, and establishing agreements between service providers and consumers. In microservices, architecture governance has the following capabilities;

- There is no need for central design governance, since microservices can make their own decisions concerning its design and implementation

- Decentralized governance enables microservices to share common and reusable services

- Some of the run-time governance aspects, such as SLAs, throttling, security monitoring and service discovery, may be implemented at the API-GW level, which we are going to discuss later

Service Registry and Service Discovery

Microservices architecture entails dealing with numerous microservices, which dynamically change in location owing to their rapid development/deployment nature.

25

Therefore, to find their location during a runtime, service registry and discovery are essential.

Service registry holds the microservices instance and their location. Microservices instance is registered with the service registry on start-up and deregistered on shutdown. Clients can, therefore, find available services and their location through a service location

Service discovery is also used to find the location of an available service. It uses two mechanisms, i.e. Client-Side Discovery and Service-Side Discovery

Advantages of Microservices

Microservices comes with numerous advantages, as discussed below:

Cost effective to scale

You don't need to invest a lot to make the entire application scalable. In terms of a shopping cart, we could simply load balance the product search module and the order-processing module while leaving out less frequently used operation services, such as inventory management, order cancellation, and delivery confirmation.

Clear code boundaries

This action should match an organization's departmental hierarchies. With different departments sponsoring product development in large enterprises, this can be a huge advantage.

Easier code changes

The code is done in a way that it is not dependent on the code of other modules and is only achieving isolated functionality. If it is done right, the chances of a change in microservices affecting other microservices are very minimal.

Easy deployment

Since the entire application is more like a group of ecosystems that are isolated from each other, deployment could be done one microservices at a time, if required. Failure in any one of these would not bring the entire system down.

Technology adaptation

You could port a single microservices or a whole bunch of them overnight to a different technology without your users even knowing about it. And yes, hopefully, you don't expect us to tell you that you need to maintain those service contracts, though.

Distributed system

This comes as implied, but a word of caution is necessary here. Make sure that your asynchronous calls are used well, and synchronous ones are not really blocking the whole flow of information. Use data partitioning well. We will come to this a little later, so don't worry for now.

Quick market response

The world being competitive is a definite advantage; otherwise, users tend to quickly lose interest if you are slow to respond to new feature requests or adoption of a new technology within your system.

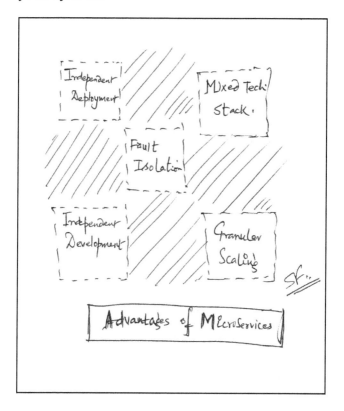

3. Understanding Microservices Architecture

Microservices have different methods of performing their functions based on their architectural style, as a standard microservices model does not exist. To understand microservices architecture, we should first analyze it in terms of service, which can be described as the basic unit in microservices. As briefly defined in chapter 1, Services are processes that communicate over a network to fulfill a goal using technology-agnostic protocols such as HTTP. Apart from technologic-agnostic protocols as a means of communication over a network, services also utilize other means of inter-process communication mechanisms, such as a shared memory for efficient communication over networks. Software developed through microservices architecture technique can be broken down into multiple component services. Each of the components in a service can be deployed, twisted according to the developer's specifications and then independently redeployed without having to develop an entirely new software application. However, this technique has its disadvantages, such as expensive remote calls, and complex procedures when redeploying and redistributing responsibilities between service components.

Services in microservices are organized around business capabilities such as user interface, front-end, recommendation, logistics, billing etc. The services in microservices can be implemented using different programming languages, databases, hardware, and software environments, depending on the developer's preferences. Microservices utilizes the cross-functional team, unlike a traditional monolith development approach where each team has a specific focus on technology layers, databases,

Uls, server-side logic or technology layers. Each team in microservices is required to implement specific products based on one or more individual service communicating via a message bus. This improves the communicability of microservices over a network between a business enterprise and the end users of their products. While most software development technique focuses on handing a piece of code to the client and in turn maintained by a team, microservices employs the use of a team who owns a product for a lifetime.

A microservices based architecture adheres to principles such as fine-grained interface, business-driven development, IDEAL cloud application architectures, polyglot programming and lightweight container deployment and DevOps with holistic service monitoring to independently deploy services. To better our understanding of microservices, we can relate it to the classic UNIX system, i.e. they receive a user request, process them, and

32

generate a response based on the query generated. Information flows in a microsystem through the dump pipes after being processed by smart endpoints.

Microservices entails numerous platforms and technologies to effectively execute their function. Microservices developers prefer to use decentralized governance over centralized governance, as it provides them with developing tools which can be used by other developers to solve emerging problems in software application development. Unlike microservices, monoliths systems utilize a single logical database across different platforms with each service managing its unique database.

The good thing about microservices is that it's a dynamic evolutionary software application technique in software application development. Therefore, it's an evolutionary design system which is ideal for the development of timeless applications which is compatible through future technologically sophisticated devices. In summary, Microservices functions by using services to componentized software applications, thereby ensuring efficient communication between applications and users over a network to fulfill an intended goal. The services are fine-grained and the protocols lightweight to break applications into small services to improve modularity and enable users to easily understand the functionality, development, and testing of the application software.

How Microservices Architecture Functions

Just like in programming, microservices have a wide range of functionality depending on the developer's choice. Microservices architecture functions by structuring applications into components or libraries of loosely coupled services, which are fine-grained and the protocols lightweight. But to understand its functionality, we should first look at Conway's law.

Conway's Law

A computer programmer named Melvin Conway came up a law in 1967 which states that "organizations which design system...are constrained to produce designs which are copies of the communication structure of these organization". This means that for a software module to function effectively there should be frequent communication between the authors. Social boundaries within an organization are reflected through the software interface structure within the application. Conway's law is the basic principle of the functionality of microservices and highlights the dangers of trying to enforce an application design that does not match the organizational requirements. To understand this, let's use an example: an organization having two departments i.e. accounting and customer support departments, whose application system are obviously interconnected. A problem arises that the accounting is overworked and cannot handle numerous tasks of processing both dissatisfied customer refunds and credit their accounts while the customer support department is underworked and very idle. How can the organization solve this problem? This is where microservices architecture comes in! The roles and responsibilities of each department in the interconnected system are split accordingly to improve customer satisfaction and minimize business losses in the organization.

In splitting the roles and responsibilities of each department, Interface Separation Principle is essential when implementing microservices to solve this problem. A typical approach isolating issues of concern in an organization through microservices is to find a communication point in the software application, then link the application by drawing a "dotted line" between the two halves of the system. However, this technique, if not carefully carried out, leads to smaller growing monoliths, which leads to isolation of important codes on the wrong side of the barrier.

Avoiding Monoliths in Microservices architecture application

Accidental monoliths are common problems when developing software applications using microservices architecture. An application may become infected with unhealthy interdependencies when service boundaries are blurred, and one service can start using the data source interface of another or even for code related to a certain logic or function to be spread over multiple places due to accidental monoliths which grow with time. This can be avoided by establishing the edge of developed application software graph.

Key Points in the Working of Microservices Architecture

- Its programming of the modern

era, where we are expected to follow the SOLID principles. It's object-oriented programming (OOP).

• It is the best way to expose the functionality of other or external components in a way that any other programming language will be able to use the functionality without adhering to any specific user interfaces, that is, services (web services, APIs, rest services, and so on).

• The whole system works according to a type of collaboration that is not interconnected or interdependent.

• Every component is liable for its own responsibilities. In other words, components are responsible for only one functionality.

• It segregates code with a separation concept, and the segregated code is reusable.

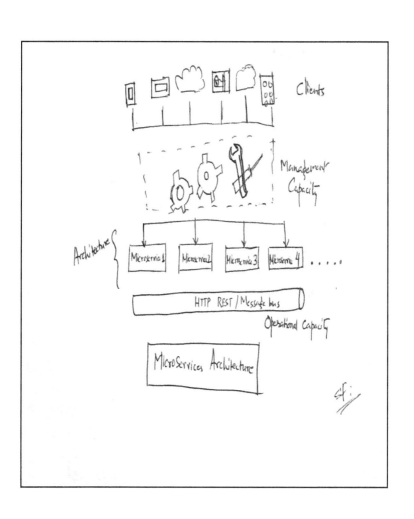

39

4. Building Microservices

We have introduced and described the functionality of microservices. In this chapter, we are going to discuss how to build microservices by separating them from the existing system and creating separate services for products and orders which can be deployed independently. First, we will begin by discussing the core concepts, programming languages, and tools that can be used to build microservices.

C#

In 2002, Microsoft developed the C# programming language and the latest release is the C# 7.0. C# is an object-oriented language and component oriented, with features like Deconstructors, ValueTuple, pattern matching, and much more.

Java Programming Language

Java is a general-purpose programming language that is concurrent, class-based, object-oriented and designed to have few implementation dependencies as possible to let application developers "write once, run anywhere" (WORA), meaning that it can run on all platforms that support Java.

Entity Framework Core

Entity framework core is a cross-platform version of Microsoft Entity Framework and can be used as a tool to build microservices. It is one of the most popular object-relational mappers (ORMs). ORM can be defined as a technique to query and manipulate data as per required business output.

.Net Framework

Developed by Microsoft, .NetFramework is a software framework that runs on Microsoft Windows with Framework Class Library to provide language interoperability across several

41

programming languages. Programs are written for .NET Framework execute software environment, rather than hardware environment, or Common Language Runtime(CLR)

Visual Studio 2017

Visual Studio 2017 is an Integrated Development Environments (IDE) developed by Microsoft to enable software application developers to build applications using various programming languages, such as Java, C#, and many more.

Microsoft SQL Server

Microsoft SQL Server(MSSQL) is a software application that has a relational database software management system which is used to store and retrieve data as requested by other software applications. It can be used in the management of microservices and it is able to communicate across a network.

Aspects of Building Microservices

To build microservices, we should first look at the important aspects, such as size and services to ensure their effective functionality after separating them from the main system.

Size of microservices

In building microservices, the first step is to break or decompose applications or systems into smaller segments or functionalities of the main application known as services. Factors to consider for high-level isolation of microservices are discussed below.

Risk due to requirement changes

It is important to note that a change in one microservice should be independent of the other microservices. Therefore, software should be isolated into smaller components termed as services in a way that if there are any requirement changes in one service, they will be independent from other microservices.

Changes in Functionality

In building microservices, we isolate functionalities that are rarely changed from the dependent functionalities that can be frequently modified. For example, in our application, the customer module notification functionality will rarely change. But its related modules, such as Order, are more likely to have frequent business changes as part of their life cycle.

Team changes

We should also consider isolating modules in such a way that one team can work independently of all the other teams. If the process of making a new developer productive—regarding the tasks in such modules—is not dependent on people outside the team, it means we are well placed.

Technology changes

Technology use needs to be isolated vertically within each module. A module should not be dependent on a technology or component from another module. We should strictly isolate the modules developed in different technologies, or stacks, or look at moving them to a common platform as the last resort.

In building microservices, the primary goal is to isolate services from the main application system and keep it as small as possible.

Features of a good Service

A good service is essential in the buildingof a good microservices architecture. A good service that can be easily used and maintained by developers and users should have the following characteristics.

Standard Data Formats

A good service should follow standardized data formats, while exchanging services or systems with other components. Most popular data formats used in the.Netstack are XML and JSON

45

Standard communication protocol

Good services should adhere to standard communication formats such as SOAP and REST.

Loose coupling

Coupling refers to the degree of direct knowledge that one service has of another. Therefore, loosely coupled means that they should not have little knowledge of the other service, so that a change in one service will not impact the other service.

Domain -Driven Design in building Microservices

Domain-Driven Design (DDD) is a technique in designing complex systems and can be useful in designing and building microservices. DDD can be described as a blueprint used to build microservices and, once it's done, a microservices can implement it just the way an application implements, let's say, an order service or an inventory service.

The main principle in domain design is to draft a model which can be written in any programming language after understanding an exact domain problem. A domain driven model, should be reusable, loosely coupled, independently designed, and should be easily isolated from a software application without having to deploy a new system.

After building microservices from a domain-based model. It is important to ensure that the size of the microservices is small enough. This can be done by having a baseline for the maximum number of domain objects which can communicate to each other. You can also do this by verifying the size all interfaces and classes in each microservices. Another way of ensuring a small size of microservices is by achieving the correct vertical isolation of services. You can then deploy each of the services independently. By deploying each service independently, we allow the host in an application to perform its independent process which is beneficial in harnessing the power of the cloud and other hybrid models of hosting.

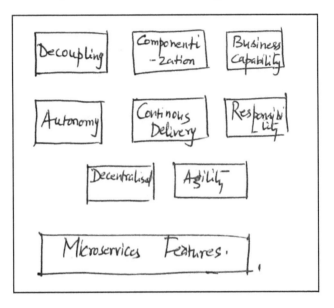

Building Microservices from Monolithic Application

As discussed earlier, the functionality in microservices lies in the isolation of services from the rest of application system translating into advantages discussed in *chapter 1*such as code reusability, independent deployment and easier code maintenance. Building microservices from monolithic application needs thorough planning. Many software architects have different approaches when it comes to transiting from monoliths to microservices, but the most important thing to consider is a correct method, as there is a possibility microservices failing to carry out their function when translated from monolith application using a wrong method. Some of the factors to consider when building microservices from the monolithic application are discussed below:

Module interdependency

When building microservices from the monolithic application, the starting point should always be to identify and pick up those parts of the monolithic application that are least dependent on other modules and have the least dependent on them. This part of the application is essential in identifying isolating application codes from the rest of the system, thereby becoming a part of the microservices which are then deployed independently in the final stage of the process. This small part of the application is referred as seams.

Technology

Technology in the form of an application's base framework is important in achieving this process. Before choosing a software framework, such as the ones discussed in this chapter, you should first identify their features. Building microservices is heavily dependent on data structures, inter-process communication being performed, and the activity of report generation. In this regard, a developer should therefore choose a framework that has great features and is ahead in technology, as they enable them to perform the transition correctly

Team structure

Team structure is important in the transition, as they are the workforce in building microservices. Teams greatly differ based on the geographical location, security of the company, and their technical skills. For the team to optimize their productivity in building microservices, they should be able to work independently. Furthermore, the team should safeguard the intellectual property of the company in developing a microservices based application.

Database

The database is considered the biggest asset of a system and their domain is defined by database tables and stored procedure. Contrary to most misconceptions, building microservices from the monolithic application does not involve dividing the whole database at once, but rather a step-by-step procedure. First, a database structure used to interact with the database is identified. Then the database structure is isolated into separate codes, which are then aligned with the newly defined vertical boundaries. Secondly, the underlying database structure is broken using the same method as the first step. The database change should not define the module used in the transition to microservices-style architecture, but rather the module should define the database. The database structure should relate to the modules picked in the transition to ensure ease in building microservices.

It is important to understand the types of acceptable changes in breaking down and merging a database, as not all changes can be implemented by the system due to data integrity. When restructuring a database to match the microservices architecture, removing foreign key relationship is the most important step, as microservices are designed to function independently of other services in an application. The final step in breaking database in microservices-style architecture is isolating the ORDER table from the ProductID, as they are still sharing information, i.e. loose coupling.

In summary, breaking down a database in microservices architecture style involves two important steps: Isolating the data structures in the code and removing foreign key relationships. It is important to note that splitting the database is not the final step in building microservices from monolithic applications, as there are other steps.

Transaction

After splitting the database from the steps mentioned above, the next step is to link services to the database in a way that ensures data integrity is maintained. However, not all services successfully go through a transaction to their successful databases due to several reasons, such as a communication fault within the system or insufficient quantities for the product requested in e-commerce platforms. For example, Amazon and e-commerce. These problems can be solved by orchestrating the whole transaction, record individual transactions across the service, or to cancel the entire transaction across the services in the system. However, when the transactions are planned out well in a microservices-style architecture application, this problem can beavoided

Building Microservices with Java

Building microservices in a java ecosystem includes container-less, self-contained and in-container strategies, all of which are discussed below.

Container-less microservices

Container-less microservices package the application, with all of its dependencies, into a single JAR file. This approach is very advantageous, due to the ease of starting and stopping services as necessary in scaling. A JAR file is also conveniently passed around by the team members that need it.

Self-contained microservices

Like container-fewer microservices, microservices are packaged into a single fat JAR file with the inclusion of embedded framework with optional compatible third-party libraries, such as Wildfly Swarm and Spring Boot, both of which will be discussed later in this chapter.

In-Container microservices

In-container microservices package an entire Java EE container and its service implementation in a Docker image. The container provides verified implementations through standard APIs, giving the developer the opportunity to solely focus on business functionality.

Microservices Framework for Java

Apart from the containers discussed above, building microservices in Java entails several microservices frameworks, such as Spring Boot, Jersey, Swagger, Dropwizard, Ninja

Web Framework, Play Framework, and many more. We are going to handle just a few common microservices frameworks below.

Microservices in Spring Boot

Spring Boot is one of the best microservices frameworks, since it is optimally integrated with supporting languages. You can Spring Boot on your own device via an embedded server. Spring Boot also eliminates the necessity of using Java EE containers.This is enabled through the implementation of Tomcat. Spring boot projects include:

Spring IO Platform: An enterprise-grade distribution for versioned applications.

Spring Framework: Used for transaction management, data access, dependency injection, messaging, and web apps.

Spring Cloud: Used for distributed systems and also used for building or deploying your microservices.

Spring Data: Used for microservices that are related to data access, be it map-reduce, relational or even non-relational.

Spring Batch: Used for higher levels of batch operations.

Spring Security: Used for authorization and authentication support.

Spring REST Docs: Used for documenting RESTful services.

Spring Social: Used for connecting to social media APIs.

Spring Mobile: Used for mobile Web apps.

Microservices in Dropwizard

Dropwizard combines mature and stable Java libraries in lightweight packages for use in a certain application. It uses Jetty for HTTP, Jersey for REST, and Jackson for JSON, along with Metrics,

Guava, Logback, Hibernate Validator, Apache HTTP Client, Liquibase, Mustache, Joda Time, and Freemarker. Maven is used to set up Dropbox application, after which a configuration class, an application class, a representation class, a resource class, or a health check can be created to run the applications.

Jersey

Jersey is an open source framework based on JAX-RS specifications. Jersey's applications can extend existing JAX-RS implementations with more features and utilities to make RESTful services and client development simpler and easier. Jersey is fast and easily routed, coupled with great documentation filled with examples for easy practice.

Play Framework

Play Framework provides an easier way to build, create, and deploy Web applications using Scala and Java. It is ideal for REST application that requires parallel handling of remote calls. It is one of the most used microservices frameworks with modular, and supports async. An example of code in Play Framework is shown below.

Restlet

Restlet enables developers to create fast and scalable WEB APIs that adhere to the RESTful architecture pattern discussed above. It has good routing and filtering, and it's available for Java SE/EE, OSGi, Google AppEngine, Android, and other major platforms. However, learning Restlet can be difficult due to the small number of users and the unavailability of tutorials. An example of a code in Restlet is shown below.

5. Integrating Microservices

Integrating microservices refers to interaction and communication of independent services located in a separate database within a software application. First, let us look at communication between microservices.

Communication between Microservices

Microservices communicate using an inter-process communication mechanism with two main message formats, namely binary and text. There are two kinds of inter-process communication mechanisms that microservices can be used to communicate, i.e. asynchronous messaging and synchronous request/response, both of which are discussed below.

Asynchronous Communication

This is an inter-process communication mechanism in which microservices communicate by asynchronously exchanging messages. It means that when an organizational client sends a message to a service to perform a certain task or answer a query, the service replies by sending a separate message back to the client. The messages, consisting of a title and body, are exchanged over channels with no limitation to the number of organizations and their clients sending and receiving messages. Likewise, any number of consumers can receive multiple messages from a single communication channel. There are two types of channels, namely: publish-subscribe and point-to-point channels. A point-to-point channel delivers a message to exactly one client reading from the channel, while the publish-subscribe channel delivers a common message to all the attached clients in a certain organization. Services utilize point-to-point channel to communicate directly to clients and publish-subscribe communication to interact with one too many clients attached to an organization

For instance, when a client requests a trip through an application, The Trip Management is notified and in turn notifies the Dispatch department about the new trip through a Trip Created message to a publish-subscribe channel. The Dispatcher then locates an available driver and notifies them by writing a Driver Proposed message to a publish-subscribe channel.

Some of the advantages of this type of communication include message buffering, isolating the client from the service, flexibility in client-service interactions, and explicitly in inter-process communication. However, there are certain downsides, such as additional operational costs, since the system is a separate entity and must be installed, configured, and operated separately, and the complexity of implementing request/ response-based interaction.

Synchronous, Request/Response IPC Mechanism

In this inter-process mechanism, a client sends a request to a service, which in turn processes the request and sends back a response. The client believes that the response will arrive in a timely fashion. While using synchronous IPC mechanism, one can choose various protocols to choose from, but the most common ones are REST and Thrift, as discussed below.

REST

REST is an IPC mechanism that uses HTTP to communicate. The basic in REST is a resource which can be equated to a business entity, such as a product or a customer or a collection of business objects. REST utilizes HTTP verbs referenced using a URL to manipulate resources. The key benefit of using this protocol is that it's simple and familiar and supports request/response-style communication, thereby enabling real-time communication within an organization and numerous clients. Some of the drawbacks include that the intermediary and buffer messages must all run concurrently and that the client must know the location of each service through a URL.

Thrift

An alternative to REST is the Apache Thrift, which provides a C-style IDL for defining APIs. Thrift is essential in generating client-side stubs and server-side skeletons. A thrift interface is made up of one or more services, which can return a value to implement the request/response style of interaction. Thrift also supports various message formats such, as JSON, binary, and compact binary.

Integration Patterns

We have discussed communication between microservices through synchronous and asynchronous inter-process communication, but this alone does not guarantee integration, as integration patterns are also essential in their communication. We will discuss the implementation of various integration patterns required by an application.

The API Gateway

The API gatewaysits between clients and services by acting as a reverse proxy, routing requests from clients to services. It acts as a proxy between services and client applications. The Azure API management as an example is responsible for the following functionalities.

- Accepting API calls

- Verifying API keys, JWT tokens, and certificates

- Supporting Auth through Azure AD and OAuth 2.0 access token

- Enforcing usage quotas and rate

65

limits

- Caching backend responses

- Logging call metadata for analytics purposes

To understand the integration of microservices in Azure API gateway, let's use an example of an application split into microservices, namely product service, order service, invoice service, and customer service. In this application,the Azure API will be working as an API Gateway to connect clients to services. The API gateway enables clients to access services in servers unknown to them by providing its own server address and authenticating the client's request by using a valid *Ocp-Apim-Subscription-Key*

Different API commands execute certain functions in a service, as shown in the table below:

API Resource	Description
GET /api/product	Gets a list of products
GET /api/product/{id}	Gets a product
PUT /api/product/{id}	Updates an existing product
DELETE /api/product/{id}	Deletes an existing product
POST /api/product	Adds a new product

The Event-Driven pattern

A microservice has a database per service pattern, meaning that it has an independent database for every dependent or independent service. Dependent services require a few external services or components, and internal services to function effectively. Dependent service does not work if any or all the services on which the service is dependent on do not work properly. Independent service does not require any other service to work properly, as the name suggests.

In the diagram, the event-manager could be a program which runs on a service which enables it to manage all the events of the subscribers. Whenever a specific event is triggered in the Publisher, the event-manager notifies a Subscriber.

Event Sourcing

Event sourcing pattern enables developers to publish an event whenever the state changes. The EventStore persists the events available for subscription, or as other services. In this pattern, tasks are simplified to avoid additional requirements in synchronizing the data model and business domain, thereby improving responsiveness, scalability, and

68

responsiveness in the microservices. For example, in an application having ORDERSERVICE as the services, a command issues a book for the User Interface to be ordered. ORDERSERVICE queries and populates the results with the `CreateOrder` event from the Event Store. The command handler raises an event to order the book, initiating a related operation. Finally, the system authorizes the event by appending the event to the event store.

Compensating Transactions

Compensating transactions refers to a means used to undo tasks performed in a series of steps. For instance, a service has implemented operations in a series and one or more tasks have failed. Compensating transactions is used to reverse the steps in a series.

Competing Consumers

Competing consumers is essential in processing messages for multiple concurrent consumers to receive the messages on the same channel. It enables an application to handle numerous requests from clients. It is implemented by passing a messaging system to another service through asynchronous communication.

Azure Service Bus

Azure Service Bus is an information delivery service used to enhance communication between two or more services. Azure Service Bus can be described as a means through which services communicate or exchange information. Azure Service Bus provides two main types of service, which are broken and non-broken communication. Broken communication is a real-time communication that ensures communication between a sender or a receiver, even when they are offline. In non-broken communication, the sender is not informed whether information has been received or not by the receiver.

Azure queues

Azure queues are cloud storage accounts which use Azure Table. They provide a means to queue a message between applications.

In summary, integrating microservices is through communication between services. Microservices communicate through inter-service communication, which can be synchronous or asynchronous. In asynchronous inter-process communication, API gateway is used to allow clients to communicate to services by acting as an intermediary between clients and services. Microservices also communicate through various patterns, as discussed in the chapter.

6. Testing Microservices

Testing microservices is an important way of ensuring their functionality by assessing the system, applications, or programs in different aspects to identify an erroneous code. Testing microservices varies in systems, depending on the microservices architectural style employed.

How to Test Microservices

It is easier to test a monolithic application than to test microservices, since monoliths provide implementation dependencies and short note delivery cycles. This is because testing microservices involves testing each service separately, with the test technique different for each service. Testing microservices can be challenging, since each service is designed to work independently. Therefore, they are tested individually rather than as a whole system It gets more challenging when testing is combined with continuous integration and deployment. However, these challenges can be solved by using a unit test framework. For example, Microsoft Unit Testing Framework, which provides a facility to test individual operations of independent components. These tests are run on every compilation of the code to ensure success in the test.

Testing Approach

As mentioned above, different application systems require different testing approaches. The testing strategy should be unique to a system and should be clear to everyone, including the none technical members of a team. Testing can be manual or automated and should be simple to perform by a system user. Testing approaches have the following techniques.

Proactive Testing

A testing approach that tries to fix defects before a build is created from the initial test designs

Reactive Testing

Testing is started after the completion of coding.

Testing Pyramid

To illustrate testing microservices, we use the testing pyramid. The Testing pyramid showcases how a well-designed test strategy is structured.

Testing Pyramid:

- System Tests (Top)

- Service Tests (Middle)

- Unit Tests (Bottom)

Unit Test

Unit testing involves testing small functionalities of an application based on the microservices architectural style.

Service Tests

Service tests entail testing an

independent service which communicates with another/external service

System Tests

They are end-to-end tests, useful in testing the entire system with an aspect of the user interface. System testsare expensive and slow to maintain and write, while service and unit testsare fast and less expensive.

Types of Microservices Test

There are various types of microservices test, as discussed below.

Unit Testing

Unit testing is used to test a single function in a service, thereby ensuring that the smallest piece of the program is tested. They are carried out to a verify a specific functionality in a system without having to test other components in the process. Unit testing is very complex, since the components are broken down into independent, small components that can be tested independently. A Test-Driven Development is used to perform a unit test.

Component (service) Testing

In service testing, the units(UI) are directly bypassed and the API, such as .Net Core Web API, is tested directly. Testing a service involves testing an independent service or a service interacting with an external device. A mock and stub approach is used to test a service interacting with an external service through an API gateway.

Integration Testing

Integration testing involves testing services in components working together. It is meant to ensure that the system is working together correctly as expected. For example, an application has StockService and OrderService depending on each other. Using integration testing, StockService is tested individually by ensuring it does not communicate with OrderService. This is accomplished through mock.

Contract Testing

Contract testing is a test that involves verifying response in each independent service. In this test, any service that is dependent on an external service is stubbed, therefore making it function independently. This test is essential in checking the contract of external services through consumer-driven contract, as discussed below.

Consumer-driven contracts

Consumer-driven refers to an integration pattern, which specifies and verifies interactions between clients and the application through the API gateway. It specifies the type of interactions a client is requesting with a defined format. The applications can then approve the requests through consumer-driven contract.

Performance Testing

It is a non-functional testing with the aim of ensuring the system is performing perfectly according to its features, such as scalability and reliability. Performance testing involves various techniques, as described below.

Load Testing

This technique involves testing the behavior of the application system under various conditions of a specific load, such as database load, critical transactions, and application servers

Stress Testing

It is a test where the system is exposed to regress stressing to find the upper capacity of the system. It is aimed at determining the behavior of a system in critical conditions, such as when the current load overrides the maximum load.

Soak Testing

Also called endurance testing, soak

78

testing is aimed at monitoring memory utilization, memory leaks, and other factors influencing system performance

Spike Testing

Spike testing is an approach inwhich the system is tested to ensure it can sustain the workload. It can be done by suddenly increasing the workload and monitoring system performance

End-to-end (UI/functional) testing

UI test is performed on the whole system, including the entire service and database. This test is the highest level of testing in microservices and it's mainly performed to increase the scope of testing. It includes fronted integration.

Sociable versus isolated unit Tests

Sociable tests resemble system tests and are performed to ensure that the application is running smoothly and as expected. Additionally, it tests other software in the same application environment. Isolated software, on the other hand, is performed before stubbing and mocking to perform unit testing, as discussed earlier. Unit testing can also be used to perform using stubs in concrete class

Stubs and Mocks

Stubs and mocks are the mockimplementations of objects interacting with the code when performing a test. The object can be replaced with a stub in one test and a mock on the other, depending on the intention of the test. Stubs can be referred to as inputs to the code under test, while mocks are outputs of a code under test

Summary

We have discussed that testing microservices is more challenging compared to testing monolithic applications in a .Net framework. The pyramid test concept enables us to understand and strategize the testing procedures. Unit test is used in testing small functionalities and class in a microservices application. Tests on top of the pyramid, such as end-end testing, are used to test the entire microservices application, rather than small functionalities or services in the application.

7. Deploying Microservices

Deploying microservices can also be challenging and is done through continuous integration and continuous deployment. Additionally, new technology such as toolchain technology and container technologies have proven essential in deploying microservices. In this chapter, we are going to discuss the basics of microservices deployment and the new technologies mentioned above. But first let's look at the key requirements in their deployment.

Deployment Requirement

- Ability to deploy/un-deploy services independent of other microservices

- A service must be able to, at each microservices level, ensure a given service does not receive more traffic compared to other services in the application.

- A failure in one microservices must not affect other services in the application

- Building and deploying microservices quickly

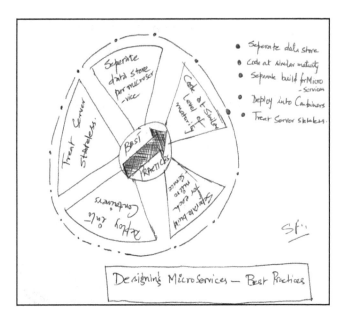

Designing MicroServices — Best Practices

Steps in Microservices Deployment

In this section, we are going to discuss the first step, i.e. Build to the final stage, which is the release stage.

Build Stage

In the build stage, a docker container is made to provide the necessary tools to create the microservices. A second container is then applied to run the built container. Then, a service source is compiled carefully to prevent errors. The services are later tested using unit testing to ensure their correspondence. The final product in this stage is a build artifact.

Continuous Integration (CI)

Any changes in the microservices build the entire application through CI. This occurs because the application code gets compiled and a comprehensive set of automated tests are run against it. CI was developed due to the problem of frequent integration. The basic idea behind CI is to ensure small changes in the software application by preserving a Delta.

Deployment

Requirements for deployment include the hardware specifications, base OS, and the correct version of a software framework. The final part is to promote the build artifacts produced in the first stage. In microservices, there is a distinction between the deployment stage and the release stage.

Continuous Deployment (CD)

In this stage, each build is deployed to the production. It is important in the deployment of microservices, as it ensures that the changes pushed to production through various lower environment work as expected in the production. This stage involves several practices, such as automated unit testing, labeling, versioning of build numbers, and traceability of changes.

Continuous Delivery

Continuous delivery is different from continuous deployment(CD) and it's focused on providing the deployment code as early as possible to the customer. In Continuous Delivery, every build is passed through quality checks to prevent errors. Continuous Delivery is implemented through automation by the build and deployment pipeline. Build and deployment pipelines ensure that a code is committed in the source repository.

Release

This is the final stage in microservices deployment and involves making a service available to possible clients. The relevant build artifact is deployed before the release of a service managed by a toggle.

Fundamentals for Successful Microservices Deployment

For microservices to be deployed successfully, the following things should be done.

Self-sufficient Teams

A team should have sufficient members with all the necessary skills and roles i.e. developers and analysts. A self-sufficient team will be able to handle development, operations, and management of microservices effectively. Smaller self-sufficient teams, who can integrate their work frequently, are precursors to the success of microservices.

CI and CD

CI and CD are essential in implementing microservices, as they automate the system to be able to push code upgrades regularly, thereby enabling the team to handle complexity by deploying microservices, as discussed above.

Infrastructure Coding

Infrastructure coding refers to representing hardware and infrastructure components, such as network servers into codes. It is important to provide deployment environments to make integration, testing, and build production possible in microservices production. It also enables developers to produce defects in lower environments. Tools such as CFEngine, Chef, Puppet, Ansible and PowerShell DSC can be used to code infrastructure. Through infrastructure coding, an infrastructure can be put under a version control system, then deployed as an artifact to enhance microservices deployment.

Utilization of Cloud Computing

Cloud computing is important in the adoption and deployment of microservices. It comes with near infinite scale, elasticity, and rapid provision capability. Therefore, it should be utilized to ensure successful deployment of microservices.

Deploying Isolated Microservices

In 2012, Adam Wiggins developed a set of principles known as a 12-factor app, which can be used to deploy microservices. According to the principles, the services are essentially stateless except for the database. These principles are applied in deploying isolated microservices as follows.

Service teams

The team should be self-sufficient and

built around services. They should be able to make the right decision to develop and support microservices decision.

Source control isolation

Source control isolation ensures that microservices do not share any source code or files in their respiratory. However, codes can be duplicated to avoid this problem.

Build Stage Isolation

Build and deploy pipelines for microservices should be isolated and separate. For isolated deployed services, build and deploy pipelines run separately. Due to this, the CI-CD tool is scaled to support different services and pipelines at a faster stage.

Release Stage Isolation

Every microservice is released in isolation with other services.

Deploy Stage Isolation

It is the most important stage in deploying isolated microservices.

Containers

Containers can be defined as pieces of software in a complete file system. Container technology is new and is now linked to the Linux world. Containers are essential in running code, runtime, system tools, and system libraries. They share their host operating system and kernel with other containers on the same host.

Deploying Microservices with Docker.

Docker is an open-source engine that lets developers and system administrators deploy self-sufficient application containers (defined above) in Linux environment. It is a great way to deploy microservices. The building deploying when starting microservices is much faster when using the Docker platform. Deploying microservices using docker is performed by following these simple steps.

- The microservices is packaged as a Docker container image

- Each service is deployed as a container

- Scaling is done based on changing the number of container instances.

Terminologies used in Docker

Docker image

A Docker image is a read-only template containing instructions for creating a Docker container. It consists of a separate file system, associated libraries, and so on. It can be composed of layers on top each other, like a layered cake. Docker images used in different containers can be reused, thereby reducing the deployment footprints of applications using the same images. A Docker image can be stored at the Docker hub.

Docker registry

Docker registry is a library of images and can either be private or public. It can also be on the same server as the Docker daemon or Docker client, or on a totally different server.

Dockerfile

A Dockerfile is a scripted file containing instructions on how to build a Docker image. The instructions are in the form multiple steps, starting from obtaining the base image.

Docker Container

Refers to a runnable instance of a Docker image.

Docker Compose

It enables a developer to define application components i.e. containers, configuration, links, volumes in a single service. A single command is then executed to establish every component in the application and run the application.

Docker Swarm

It's a Docker service in which container nodes function together. It operates as a defined number of instances of a replica task in a Docker image.

Deploying Microservices with Kubernetes

Kubernetes is a recent technology in deploying microservices. It extends Docker capabilities, since Linux containers can be managed in a single system. It also allows the management and running of Docker containers across multiple hosts offering co-location of containers, service discovery, and replication control. Kubernetes has become an extremely powerful approach in deploying microservices, especially for large-scale microservices deployments.

Summary

We have discussed that for

microservices to be deployed effectively, developers should adhere to the best deployment practices, as discussed in this chapter. Containers are effective in microservices deployment as they isolate services. Microservices can be deployed using either Docker or Kubernetes, as discussed above,

8. Security in Microservices

Securing microservices is a requirement for an enterprise running their applications or websites on microservices, since data breaches or hacking are very common these days and can lead to massive unwarranted loses. As much as security in an organization is everyone's responsibility, microservices should be secured after their deployment, as we are going to discuss in this chapter. First, let's look at security in monolithic applications.

Security in Monolithic Applications

As we discussed earlier, monolithic applications are deployed dependently, thereby they have a large surface area in an application compared to microservices. The fact that microservices are isolated from each other and deployed independently means that they are more secure, compared to monoliths. However, implementing security in microservices can be challenging. The monolithic application has different attack vectors from microservices, and their security is implemented as follows.

- Security in a typical monolithic application is about finding 'who is the intruder' and 'what can they do' and how do we propagate the information.

- After establishing this information, security is then implemented from a common security component which is at the beginning of the request handling chain. The component uses an underlying user respiratory or a store to populate the required information.

This is done through an authentication (auth) mechanism, which verifies the identity of a user and manages what they can or cannot access through permissions. Data from client to the server is then secured through encryption achieved through HTTPS protocol. In a.Net monolithic application, a user files a request to a web application through a web browser which requires them to enter their username and password. This request is then transferred through HTTPS and load balancer to the Auth, which then connects to the user credential store container, such as SQL server, which contains login details of various users. The user-supplied credentials i.e. username and password, are then verified against the ones retrieved from credentials store by the auth layer.

On verification, the user's browser automatically creates a cookie session, enabling him or her to access the requested information. In this kind of monolithic application, security is achieved by ensuring that the application modules do not separate verification and validation of request while communicating with each other.

Security in Microservices

Security in microservices architecture is achieved by translating the pattern used in securing monolithic applications to microservices. In microservices, the authentication layer is broken into microservices in different applications, which will need its authentication mechanisms. The user credential store is different for every microservices. From our previous discussion, this pattern cannot be implemented, since auth cannot be synced across all devices, and validating inter-process communication might be impossible. Additionally, modern applications based on Android or iOS cannot support secure information between clients and services, since session-based authentication using cookies is not possible, as in monolithic applications.So, the question is how these problems are solved to secure microservices application. The solution comes in the form of OpenID Connect, JSON Web Tokens and OAuth 2.0, as we will discuss below.

JSON Web Tokens

JSON Web Tokens(JWT) is used in producing a data structure which contains information about the issuer and the recipient, along with the sender's identity. They can be deployed independently, irrespective of OAuth 2.0 or OPENID Connect, as they are not tied together. The tokens are secured with symmetric and asymmetric keys to ensure information received by a client is authentic or trustable.

The OAuth 2.0

The OAuth 2.0 is an authorization framework that lets a third-party application to obtain finite access to a HTTP service, either on behalf of the resource owner by orchestrating an approval interaction between the resource owner and the HTTP service, or by allowing the third-party application to obtain access on its behalf. OAuth 2.0 functions as a delegated authorization framework, relying on authentication mechanisms to complete authorization framework. The figure below illustrates the functionality of OAuth in securing microservices.

OpenID Connect

It comes top of OAuth 2.0 protocol and its importance in the user authentication i.e. standard for authentication. It allows a client to verify end users based on the authentication performed by an authorization server. It is also used to obtainthe basic profile information of end users. Clients using any device, i.e. web-based, mobile and javascript can access information relating to authenticated sessions and end users through OpenID Connect. Validation of the end user is through sending ID token to an application used by a client.

To understand microservices security, let's use an example of a client requesting a service through his/ her mobile-based microservices application.

OAuth and the OpenID Connect (Authorization Server)authenticates the client to access data in the microservices by issuing the Access Token. The API Gateway is the only entry to the application's microservices, then receives the Access Token along with the client's request. The Token Translation at the API Gateway extracts the Access token from the client's request and sends it to the authorization server to retrieve the JSON Web Tokens. JSON tokens, along with the client's request, are then passed to the microservices layer by the API Gateway. JSON Web Token contains the necessary information used in storing user sessions. At each microservices layer, there are components used to process the JSON tokens, thereby obtaining the client's request and its information.

Other Security Practices

There are other practices to secure microservices apart from OAuth 2.0 and Open ID connect, as we are going to discuss below.

Standardization of libraries and frameworks

This refers to introducing libraries and frameworks in the development process. It is done to ease out patching, in case of any vulnerability found. It also minimizes the risk introduced by ad hoc implementation of libraries or tools around development.

Regular vulnerability Identification and mitigation

The vulnerability is regularly checked using an industry-standard vulnerability scanner to scan the source code, coupled with binaries and the findings addressed accordingly.

Third-party audits and penetration testing.

External audits and penetration test are

conducted regularly as they are essential in ensuring data integrity in applications or websites involving sensitive critical data or information

Logging and monitoring

Logging is useful in detecting and recovering from hacking attacks by aggregating logs from different systems and services, thereby essential in microservices security.

Network Segregation

Network segregation or partitioning, although only possible in the monolithicapplication, can be effective in ensuring the security of microservices. This can be achieved through the creation of different network segments and subnets.

Summary

We have discussed that securing microservices is essential to any organization having microservices application systems. Security patterns in

104

a monolithic application cannot be implemented in microservices application due to incompatibility problems, such as each microservices requiring their own authentication mechanism and so on, as discussed in this chapter. Therefore, secure token-based approaches such as OAuth 2.0 and OpenID Connect can be used to secure microservices through authorization and authentication.

9. Criticism and Case Study

The emergence of microservices as a technique in software application development has been largely criticized for some reasons, namely:

- Information barriers due to services

- Communication of services over a network is costly in terms of network latency and message processing time

- Complexity in testing and deployment

- Difficulty in moving responsibilities between services. It involves communication between different teams, rewriting the functionality in another language or fitting it into a different infrastructure.

- Too many services, if not deployed correctly, may slow system performance.

- Additional complexity, such as network latency, message formats, load balancing and fault tolerance.

Nano service

Nano service refers to anti-patterns where a service is too fine-grained, meaning that the overheads outweighs its utility. Microservices have continually been criticized as a Nano service due to numerous problems such as the code overhead, runtime overhead, and fragmented logic. However, there are some proposed alternatives to the Nano service. These are:

- Packaging the functionality as software library rather than a service.

- Combining the functionality with other functionalities to produce a more substantial useful service

- Refactoring the system by putting the functionality in other services or redesigning the system altogether.

Design for Failure

Microservices have been criticized as prone to failure compared to monoliths, since they introduce isolated services to the system, which increases the possibility of having a system failure. Some of the reasons that may lead to failure in microservices include network instability and unavailability of the underlying resources. However, there are certain design mechanisms that may ensure an unavailable or unresponsive microservices does not cause the whole application to fail. It ensures that microservices is fault tolerant and swiftly recovers after experiencing a failure. In microservices, it is important to maintain real-time monitoring, since services can fail at any time. The failures should be repaired quickly to be able to restore the services. Let's discuss common ways of avoiding failure in microservices application.

108

Circuit Breaker

A circuit breaker is a fault monitor component which is configured to each service in the application. The fault monitor then observes service failures, and when they reach a certain threshold, the circuit breaker stops any further requests to the services. This is essential in avoiding unnecessary resource consumption by requesting delay timeouts. It is also important in monitoring the whole system.

Bulkhead

Since microservices applications comprise of numerous services, a failure in one service may affect the functioning of other microservices, or even the entire application. Bulkhead is essential in preventing a failure in one microservices from affecting the whole application, as it isolates different parts of the microservices application

Timeout

Timeout is a pattern mechanism to

prevent clients from overwaiting for a response from microservices once they have sent as a request through there devices. Clients configure a time interval in which they are comfortable to wait for increasing efficiency and client satisfaction.

These patterns are configured to the API Gateway, and monitors the response of the microservices once they receive a request. When a service is unresponsive or unavailable, the Timeout mechanism notifies the user to try accessing the microservices another time to avoid overloading the application system and prevent failure in one service from affecting the other microservices. Additionally, the Gateway can be used as the central point to monitor each microservices, thereby informing developers of a failure.

Microservices Disrupting the Fintech Industries

Microservices have greatly disrupted the

Fintech industries and other sectors. By breaking down big, complex systems into smaller pieces or services, microservices allow complicated work to be divided and distributed amongst smaller teams, making it easier to develop, test, and deploy. Fintech industries are realizing that they are being disrupted and need to reinvent them to compete against these digital-only businesses. The speed of innovation is dictated by the ability to expose business assets in a digital-friendly manner, and in some instances leverage external assets to provide a more social experience. The core paradigm enabling the use of business assets within mobile or tablet applications is through microservices. For a large majority of enterprises, microservices have become a new business channel to expose key assets, data, or services for consumption by mobile, web, internet of things, and enterprise applications. It can represent monetary benefit by metering usage of API services, and providing different plans (i.e. Gold, Silver Bronze) at various price-points, or simply making them available at no-charge to increase usage and brand promotion through increased marketing.

Companies using Microservices

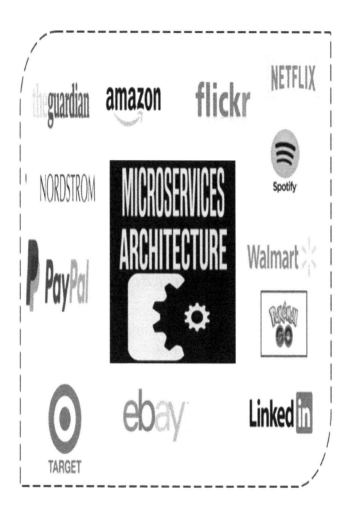

10. Summary

We have discussed a lot about microservices from their invention, definition, advantages, building, integration techniques, deployment, and finally their security. In this chapter, we are going to recap what we have already discussed.

Before Microservices?

As we had discussed, before the invention of microservices, monolithic architecture and Service-Oriented Architecture was used to develop software applications

Monolithic Architecture

Monolithic architecture consists of components such as user interface, business logic, and database access, which are interconnected and interdependent. Therefore, a minor change inany module of the application results in a change to the entire application. This would require the redeployment of the entire application. Monolithic architecture has numerous challenges, including code complexity, scalability, large interdependent code, and difficulty in the adoption of a new technology in terms of application or new devices.

Service-oriented architecture

Service-oriented architecture is an improvement of monolithic architecture resolving some of the challenges we mentioned above. Services primarily started with SOA and it's the main concept behind it. As we have already defined, a service is a piece of program or code providing some functionality to the system components. SOA comes with some advantages, such as the ability to reuse codes, and the ability to upgrade applications without necessarily deploying the entire application.

Microservices architecture.

Microservices architecture is very similar to SOA, except that services are deployed independently. A change in a piece of program or code does not change the functionality of the entire application. For services to function independently, a certain discipline and strategy are required. Some of the disadvantages we discussed include clear boundaries, easy deployment, technology adaptation, affordable scalability, and quick market response.

Building Microservices from Monoliths

We discussed building microservices from an existing monolithic application. First is to identify decomposition candidates within a monolith based on parameters including code complexity, technology adaptation, resource requirement, and human dependency. Second is the identification of seams, which act as boundaries in microservices, then the separation can start. Seams should be picked on the right parameters depending on module interdependency, team structure, database. and existing technology. The master database should be handled with care through a separate service or configuration. An advantage of microservices having its own database is that it removes many of the existing foreign key relationships, thereby has a high transaction-handling ability.

Integration Techniques

Microservices integration techniques are mainly based on communication between microservices. We discussed that there are two ways in which microservices communicate: synchronous and asynchronous communication. Synchronous communication is based on request/response, while asynchronous style is event-based. Integration patterns are essential to facilitate complex interaction among microservices. We discussed integrating microservices using event-driven patterns in the API Gateway. The event-driven pattern works by some services publishing their events, and some subscribing to those available events. The subscribing services simply react independently to the event-publishing services, based on the event and its metadata.

Deployment.

We discussed microservices deployment and how it can be challenging for various reasons. Breaking the central database further increases the overall challenges. Microservices deployment requires continuous delivery(CD) and continuous integration (CI) right from the initial stages. Infrastructure can be represented with codes for easy deployment using tools such as CFEngine, Chef, Puppet, and PowerShell DSC. Microservices can be deployed using Docker or Kubernetes after containerization.

Testing microservices

We discussed the test pyramid representing the types of test. Unit test is used to verify small functionalities in the entire application, while system test is used to verify the entire application on its functionality. The mock and stub approach is used in microservices testing. This approach makes testing independent of other microservices and eliminates challenges in testing the application's database due to mock database interactions. Integration testing is concerned with external microservices communicating with them in the process. This is done through mocking external services.

Security

Securing microservices is essential to an organization to ensure data integrity. In a monolithic application, security is attained through having a single point of authentication and authorization. However, this approach is not possible in microservices architecture, since each service needs to be secured independently. Therefore, the OAuth 2.0 authorization framework, coupled with OpenID Connect, is used to secure microservices. OAuth 2.0's main role is to authorize clients into the application system as we discussed in *chapter 7*. One provider of OAuth 2.0 and OpenID Connect is the Azure Active Directory (Azure AD)

Conclusive Remarks

It is our hope that this book has been essential in your understanding of the microservices architecture by answering all your questions based on this wide subject. Microservices architecture is a pretty new concept, and is still in development. Therefore, the contents of this book may change overtime.

My Other Books available across the platforms in e-book, paperback and audible versions:

1. **Blockchain Technology : Introduction to Blockchain Technology and its impact on Business Ecosystem**

2. DevOps Handbook: Introduction to DevOps and its Impact on Business Ecosystem

3. Blockchain Technology and DevOps : Introduction and

Impact on Business Ecosystem

4. Love Yourself: 21 day plan for learning "Self-Love" to

cultivate self-worth ,self-belief, self-confidence & happiness

LOVE YOURSELF

21 day plan for learning "Self Love"
to cultivate self-worth, self-belief,
self-confidence & happiness

STEPHEN FLEMING

5. Intermittent Fasting: 7 effective techniques of Intermittent Fasting

7 EFFECTIVE TECHNIQUES OF

INTERMITTENT FASTING

**Stay Healthy,Lose Weight,
Slow Down Aging Process & Live Longer!**

STEPHEN FLEMING

6. Love Yourself and intermittent Fasting(Mind and Body Bundle Book)

You can check all my Books on my **Amazon's Author Page**

** If you prefer audible versions of these books, I have few free coupons, mail me at valueadd2life@gmail.com. If available, I would mail you the same.

Book 2: Kubernetes Handbook

A Non-Programmer's Guide

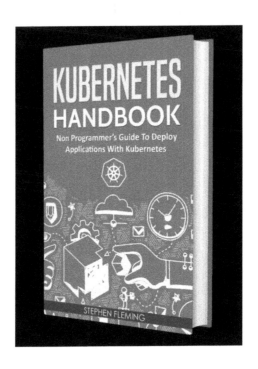

Copyright © 2018 Stephen Fleming

BONUS TECHNOLOGY BOOKLET

Dear Friend,
I am privileged to have you onboard. You have shown faith in me and I would like to reciprocate it by offering the maximum value with an amazing booklet which contains latest technology updates on DevOps and Blockchain.

"Get Instant Access to Free Booklet and Future Updates"

- Link: http://eepurl.com/dge23r

OR

- QR Code : You can download a QR code reader app on your mobile and open the link:

Preface

This book has been well written as a guide to *getting started with Kubernetes, how they operate and how they are deployed*.

The book also explains the features and functions of Kubernetes and how it can be integrated into a total operational strategy for any project.

Additionally, the reader will be able to learn how to deploy real-world applications with Kubernetes.

The book has been written in a simple, easy to comprehend language and can be used by Non-Programmers, Project Managers, Business Consultants or any other persons with an interest in Kubernetes.

1. Introduction

Kubernetes Defined

Kubernetes, also known as K8s is an open-source container-orchestration system that can be used for programming deployment, scaling, and management of containerized applications. Kubernetes were innovated with the aim of providing a way of automatically deploying, scaling and running operations of container applications across a wide range of hosts. A container is a standalone, lightweight and executable package of a part of the software that is composed of components required to run it, i.e., system tools, code, runtime, system libraries, and settings. Containers function to segregate software from its adjacentenvironment, i.e., for instance, variances in development and staging environments thereby enabling the reduction of conflicts arising when teams run separate software on the same network infrastructure.

Containers may be flexible and really fast, attributed to their lightweight feature, but they are prone to one problem: they have a short lifespan and are fragile. To overcome this enormous problem and increase the stability of the whole system, developers utilize Kubernetes to schedule and orchestrate container systems instead of constructing each small component, making up a container system bullet-proof. With Kubernetes, a container is easily altered and re-deployed when misbehaving or not functioning as required.

Kubernetes Background

The initial development of Kubernetes can be attributed to engineers working in industries facing analogous scaling problems. They started experimenting with smaller units of deployment utilizing cgroups and kernel namespaces to develop a process of individual deployment. With time, they developed containers which faced limitations, such that they were fragile, leading to a short lifetime; therefore, Google came up with an innovation calling it Kubernetes, a Greek name meaning "pilot" or "helmsman" in an effort aimed at sharing their own infrastructure and technology advantage with the community at large. The earliest founders were Joe Beda, Brendan Burns and Craig McLuckie who were later joined by Tim Hockin and Brian Grant from Google. In mid-2014, Google announced the development of Kubernetes based on its Borg System, unveiling a wheel with seven spokes as its logo which each wheel spoke representing a nod to the project's code name. Google released Kubernetes v1.0, the first version of their development on July 21, 2015, announcing that they had partnered with Linux Foundation to launch the Cloud Native Computing Foundation (CNCF) to promote further innovation and development of the Kubernetes. Currently, Kubernetes provides organizations with a way of effectively dealing with some of the main management and operational concerns faced in almost all organizations worldwide, by offering a solution for administration and managing several containers deployed at scale, eliminating the practice of just working with Docker on a manually-configured host.

Advantages Of KUBERNETES

While Kubernetes was innovated to offer an efficient way of working with containers on Google systems, it has a wider range of functionalities and can be used essentially by anyone regardless of whether they are using the Google Compute Engine on Android devices. They offer a wide range of advantages, with one of them being the combination of various tools for container deployments, such as orchestration, services discovery and load balancing. Kubernetes promotes interaction between developers, providing a platform for an exchange of ideas for the development of better versions. Additionally, Kubernetes enables the easy discovery of bugs in containers due to its beta version.

2. How Kubernetes Operates

Kubernetes design features a set of components referred to as primitives which jointly function to provide a mechanism of deploying, maintaining and scaling applications. The components are loosely coupled with the ability to be extensible to meet a variety of workloads. Extensibility is attributed to the Kubernetes API, which is utilized by internal components coupled with extensions and containers that operates on Kubernetes. In simple, understandable terms, Kubernetes is basically an object store interacting with various codes. Each object has three main components: the metadata, a specification and a current status that can be observed; therefore, a user is required to provide metadata with a specification describing the anticipated state of the objects. Kubernetes will then function to implement the request by reporting on the progress under the status key of the object.

The Kubernetes architecture is composed of various pieces which work together as an interconnected package. Each component at play has a specified role, some of which are discussed below. Additionally, some components are placed in the container/cloud space.

- **Master**- It is the overall managing component which runs one or more minions.

- **Minion** –Operatesunder the master to accomplish the delegated task.

- **Pod**- A piece of application responsible for running a minion. It is also the basic unit of manipulation in Kubernetes.

- **Replication Controller**- Tasked with confirming that the requested number of pods are running on minions every time.

- *Label*- Refers to a key used by the Replication Controller for service discovery.

- *Kubecfg*- A command line used to configure tools.

- *Service*- Denotes an endpoint providing load balancing across a replicated group of pods.

With these components, Kubernetes operate by generating a master which discloses the Kubernetes API, in turn, allowing a user to request the accomplishment of a certain task. The master then issues containers to perform the requested task. Apart from running a Docker, each node is responsible for running the Kubelet service whose main function is to operate the container manifest and proxy service. Each of the components is discussed in detail in this chapter.

Docker and Kubernetes

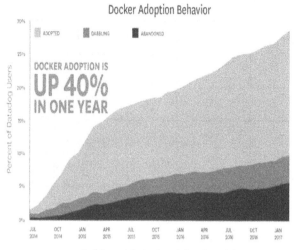

Docker Adoption Behavior

While Docker and Kubernetes may appear similar and help users run applications within containers, they are very different and operate at different layers of the stack, and can even be used together. A Docker is an open source package of tools that help you "Build, Ship, and Run" any app anywhere, and also enables you to develop and create software with containers. The use of a Docker involves the creation of a particular file known as a Dockerfile which defines a build process and produces a Docker image when the build process is integrated to the 'Docker build' command. Additionally, Docker offers a cloud-based repository known as the Docker Hub which can be used to store and allocate the created container images. Think of it like GitHub for Docker Images. One limitation involved in the use of Docker is that a lot of work is involved in running multiple containers across multiple devices when using microservices. For instance, the process involves running the right containers at the right time; therefore, you have to work out how the containers will communicate with each other, figure out storage deliberations and handle or redeploy failed containers or hardware. All this work could be a nightmare, especially when you are doing it manually; therefore, the need for Kubernetes.

Unlike Docker, Kubernetes is an open-source container orchestration platform which allows lots of containers to harmoniously function together automatically, rather than integrating every container separately across multiple machines, thus cutting down the operational cost involved. Kubernetes has a wide range of functions, some of which are outlined below:

- Integrating containers across different machines.

- Redeploying containers on different machines in case of system failure.

- Scaling up or down based on demand changes by adding or removing containers.

- They are essential in maintaining the consistent storage of multiple instances of an application.

- Important for distributing load between containers.

As much as Kubernetes is known for container management, Docker also can manage containers using its own native container management tool known as Docker Swarm, which enables you to independently deploy containers as Swarms which then interact as a single unit. It is worth noting that Kubernetes interacts only with the Docker engine itself and never with Docker Swarm.

As mentioned above, Kubernetes can be integrated with the Docker engine with an intention of co-ordinating the development and execution of Docker containers on Kubelet. In this type of integration, the Docker engine is tasked with running the actual container image built by running 'Docker build.' Kubernetes, additionally, handles higher level concepts, including service-discovery, load balancing, and network policies.

Interestingly, as much as Docker and Kubernetes are essentially different from their core, they can be used concurrently to efficiently develop modern cloud architecture by facilitating the management and deployment of containers in the distributed architecture.

Containers are the new packaging format because they're efficient and portable

- App Engine supports Docker containers as a custom runtime
- Google Container Registry: private container image hosting on GCS with various CI/CD integrations
- Compute Engine supports containers, including managed instance groups with Docker containers
- The most powerful choice is a container **orchestrator**

Pods: Running Containers in Kubernetes

Pods area group of containers and volumes which share the same resource - usually an IP address or a filesystem, therefore allowing them to be scheduled together. Basically, a pod denotes one or more containers that can be controlled as a single application. A pod can be described as the most basic unit of an application that can be used directly with Kubernetes and consists of containers that function in close association by sharing a lifecycle and should always be scheduled on the same node. Coupled containers condensed in a pod are managed completely as a single unit and share various components such as the environment, volumes and IP space.

Generally, pods are made into two classes of containers: a main container which functions to achieve the specified purpose of the workload and some helper containers which can optionally be used to accomplish closely-related tasks. Pods are tightly tied to the main application, however, some applications may benefit by being run and managed in their containers. For instance, a pod may consist of one container running the primary application server and a helper container extracting files to the shared file system, making an external repository detect the changes. Therefore, on the pod level, horizontal scaling is generally discouraged as there are other higher level tolls best suited for the task.

146

It is important to note that Kubernetes schedules and orchestrates functionalities at the pod level rather than the container level; therefore, containers running in the same pod have to be managed together in a concept known as the shared fate which is key in the underpinning of any clustering system. Also, note that pods lack durability since the master scheduler may expel a pod from its host by deleting the pod and creating a new copy or bringing in a new node.

Kubernetes assigns pods a shared IP enabling them to communicate with each other through a component called a localhost address, contrary to Docker configuration where each pod is assigned a specific IP address.

Users are advised against managing pods by themselves as they do not offer some key features needed in an application, such as advanced lifecycle management and scaling. Users are instead invigorated to work with advanced level objects which use pods or work with pod templates as base components to implement additional functionality.

Replication and Other Controllers

Before we discuss replication controllers and other controllers, it is important to understand Kubernetes replication and its uses. To begin with, being a container management tool, Kubernetes was intended to orchestrate multiple containers and replication. Replication refers to creating multiple versions of an application or container for various reasons, including enhancing reliability, load balancing, and scaling. Replication is necessary for various situations, such as in microservices-based applications to provide specific functionality, to implement native cloud applications and to develop mobile applications. Replication controllers, replica sets, and deployments are the forms of replications and are discussed below:

Replication Controller

A replication controller is an object that describes a pod template and regulates controls to outline identical replicas of a pod horizontally by increasing or decreasing the number of running copies. A Replication controller provides an easier way of distributing load across the containers and increasing availability natively within Kubernetes. This controller knows how to develop new pods using a pod template that closely takes after a pod definition which is rooted in the replication controller configuration.

The replication controller is tasked to ensure that the number of pods deployed in a cluster equals the number of pods in its configuration. Thus, in case of failure in a pod or an underlying host, the controller will create new pods to replace the failed pods. Additionally, a change in the number of replicas in the controller's configuration, the controller will either initiate or kill containers to match the anticipated number. Replication controllers are also tasked to carry out rolling updates to roll over a package of pods to develop a new version, thus minimizing the impact felt due to application unavailability.

Replication Sets

Replication sets are an advancement of replication controller design with greater flexibility with how the controller establishes the pods requiring management. Replication sets have a greater enhanced replica selection capability; however, they cannot perform rolling updates in addition to cycling backends to a new version. Therefore, replication sets can be used instead of higher level units which provide similar functionalities.

Just like pods, replication controllers and replication sets cannot be worked on directly as they lack some of the fine-grained lifecycle management only found in more complex tools.

Deployments

Deployments are meant to replace replication controls and are built with replication sets as the building blocks. Deployments offer a solution to problems associated with the implementation of rolling updates. Deployments are advanced tools designed to simplify the lifecycle of replicated pods. It is easy to modify replication by changing the configuration which will automatically adjust the replica sets, manage transitions between different versions of the same application, and optionally store records of events and reverse capabilities automatically. With these great features, it is certain that deployment will be the most common type of replication tool used in Kubernetes.

Master and Nodes

Initially, minions were called nodes, but their names have since been changed back to minions. In a collection of networked machines common in data centers, one machine hosts the working machines. The working machines are known as nodes. The master machine is responsible for running special co-ordinating software that schedules containers on the nodes. A collection of masters and nodes are known as clusters. Masters and nodes are defined by the software component they run. The master is tasked to run three main items:

- API Server - The API server ensures that all the components on the master and nodes achieve their respective tasks by making API calls.

- Etcd - This is a service responsible for keeping and replicating the current configuration and run the state of the cluster. It is implemented as a lightweight distributed key-value store.

- Scheduler and Controller Manager- These processes schedule containers, specifically pods, onto target nodes. Additionally, they may correct numbers of the running processes.

A node usually carries out three important processes, which are discussed below:

- Kubelet- It is an advanced background process (daemon) that runs on each node and functions to respond to commands from the master to create, destroy and monitor containers on that host.

- Proxy - It is a simple network proxy that can be used to separate the IP address of a target container from the name of the services it provides.

- cAdvisor- It is an optional special daemon that collects, aggregates, processes, and exports information about running containers. The information may exclude information on resource isolation, historical usage, and key network statistics.

The main difference between a master and a node is based on the set of the process being undertaken.

The 10,000-foot view

users   master   nodes

Services

A service assigns a fixed IP to your pod replicas and allows other pods or services to communicate with them

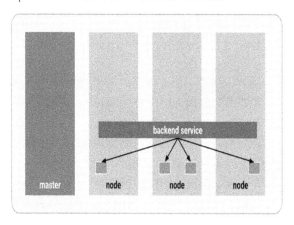

In Kubernetes, a service is an important component that acts a central internal load balancer and representatives of the pods. Services can also be defined as a long-lasting, well-known endpoint that points to a set of pods in a cluster. Services consist of three critical components: an external IP address (known as a portal, or sometimes a portal IP), a port and a label selector. Service is usually revealed through a small proxy process. The service proxy is responsible for deciding which pod to route to an endpoint request via a label selector. It also acts as a thin look-up service to determine a way of handling the request. The service proxy is, therefore, in simple terms, a tuple that maps a portal, port, and label selector.

A service abstraction is essential to allow you to scale out or replace the backend work units as necessary. A service's IP address remains unchanged and stable regardless of the changes to the pods it routes too. When you deploy a service, you are simply gaining discoverability and can simplify your container designs. A service should be configured any time you need to provide access to one or more pods to another application or external consumers. For example, if you have a set of pods running web servers that should be accessible from the internet, a service will provide the necessary concept. Similarly, if a web service needs to store and recover data, an internal service is required to authorize access to the database pods.

In most circumstances, services are only

available via the use of an internally routable IP address. However, they can also be made available from their usual places through the use of several strategies, such as the NodePort configuration which works by opening a static port on each node's external networking interface. In this strategy, the traffic to the external port is routed automatically using an internal cluster IP service to the appropriate pods. Instead, the Load Balancer service strategy can be used to create an external load balancer which, in turn, routes to the services using a cloud provider's load balancer integration. The cloud controller manager, in turn, creates an appropriate resource and configures it using an internal service address. In summary, the main functionality of services in Kubernetes is to expose a pod's unique IP address which is usually not exposed outside the cluster without a service.

You can have multiple services with different configurations and features

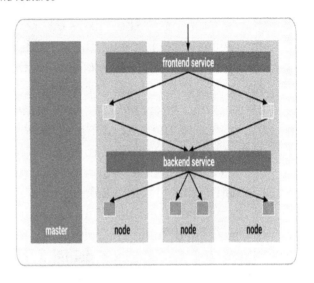

Service Discovery

Service discovery refers to the process of establishing how to connect to a service. Services need dynamically to discover each other to obtain IP addresses and port detail which are essential in communicating with other services in the cluster.Kubernetes offers two mechanisms of service discovery: DNS and environmental variable. While there is a service discovery option based on environmental variables available, most users prefer the DNS-based service discovery. Both are discussed below.

Service Discovery with Environmental Variables

This mechanism of service discovery occurs when a pod exposes a service on a node, initiating Kubernetes to develop a set of environmental variables on the exposed node to describe the new service. This way, other pods on the same node can consume it easily. Managing service discovery using environmental variable mechanism is not scalable, therefore, most people prefer the Cluster DNS to discover services.

Cluster DNS

Cluster DNS enables a pod to discover services in the cluster, thereby enabling services to communicate with each other without having to worry about IP addresses and other fragile schemes. With cluster DNS, you can configure your cluster to schedule a pod and service that expose DNS. Then, when new pods are developed, they are informed of this service and will use it for look-ups. The cluster DNS is made of three special containers listed below:

- Etcd - Important for storing all the actual look-up information.

- SkyDns- It is a special DNS server written to read from etcd.

- Kube2sky - It is a Kubernetes-specific program that watches the master for any changes to the list of services and then publishes the information into etcd. SkyDns will then pick it up.

Apart from environmental variables and cluster DNS, there are other mechanisms which you can use to expose some of the services in your cluster to the rest of the world. This mechanism includes Direct Access, DIY Load Balancing, and Managed Hosting.

Direct Access- Involves configuring the firewall to pass traffic from the outside world to the portal IP of your service. Then, the proxy located on the node selects the container requested by the service. However, direct access faces a problem of limitation where you are constrained to only one pod to service the request, therefore, fault intolerant.

DIY Load Balancing- Involves placing the load balancer in front of the cluster and then populating it with the portal IPs of your service; therefore, you will have multiple pods available for the service request.

Managed Hosting- Most cloud providers supporting Kubernetes offer an easier way to make your services discoverable. All you need to do is to define your service by including a flag named *CreateExternalLoadBalncer* and set its value to *true*. By doing this, the cloud provider automatically adds the portal IPs for your service to a fleet of load balancers that is created on your behalf.

ReplicaSets-Replica Set Theory/Hands-on with ReplicaSets

As mentioned earlier, ReplicaSets is an advanced version of Replication Controller, offering greater flexibility in how the controller establishes the pods it is meant to manage. A ReplicaSet ensures that a specified number of pod replicas are running at any given time. Deployment can be used to effectively manage ReplicaSets as it enables it to provide declarative updates to pods combined with a lot of other useful features.

Using ReplicaSets is quite easy since most Kubernetes commands supporting Replication Controllers also support ReplicaSets except the rolling update command which is best used in Deployments. While ReplicaSets can be used independent of each other, it is best used by Deployments as a mechanism of orchestrating pod creation, deletion, and updates. By using

Deployments, you will not have to worry about managing the ReplicaSets they develop as they deploy and manage their ReplicaSets.

Daemon Sets

Daemon Sets are a specialized form of pod controller which runs a copy of a pod on each node in the cluster (or a subset, if specified). Daemon Sets are useful when deploying pods which help perform maintenance and provide services for the nodes themselves by creating pods on each added node, and garbage collects pods when nodes are removed from the cluster. Daemon Sets can be used for running daemons that require running on all nodes of a cluster. Such things can be cluster storage daemons, such as Qubyte, ceph, glusterd, etc., log collectors such as Fluentd or Logstash, or monitoring daemons such as Prometheus Node Exporter, Collectd, New Relic agent, etc.

The daemon can be deployed to all nodes, but it's important to split a single daemon to multiple daemons. Note that

163

in situations involving a cluster with nodes of different hardware requiring adaption in the memory and CPU, you may have to include for the daemon for effective functionality.

There are other cases where you may require different logging, monitoring, or storage solutions on separate nodes of your cluster. In such circumstances where you prefer to deploy the daemons only to a specific set of nodes rather than the entire node, you may use a node selector to specify a subdivision of the nodes linked to the Daemon Set. For this to function effectively, you should have labeled your nodes consequently.

There are four main mechanisms in which you can communicate to the daemons discussed below:

- Push - In this mechanism, the pods are configured to push data to a service, making the services undiscoverable to clients.

- NodeIP and known port - The pods utilize a host port, enabling clients to access each NodeIP via this port.

- DNS - In this mechanism, pods are accessed via a headless service by either the use of an endpoints resource or obtaining several A Records from DNS.

- Service - The pods are accessible via the standard service. The client can access a daemon on a random node using the same service; however, in this mechanism, you may not be able to access a specific node.

Since Daemon Sets are tasked to provide essential services and are required throughout the fleet, they, therefore, are allowed to bypass pod scheduling restrictions which limit other controllers from delegating pods to certain hosts. For instance, attributed to its unique responsibilities, the master server is usually configured to be inaccessible for normal pod scheduling, providing Daemon Sets with the ability to override the limitation on the pod-by-pod basis to ensure that essential services are running.

As per now, Kubernetes does not offer a mechanism of automatically updating a node. Therefore, you can only use the semi-automatic way of updating the pods by deleting the daemon set with the −cascade=false option, so that the pods may allot on the nodes; then you can develop a new Daemon Set with an identical pod selector and an updated pod template. The new Daemon Set will automatically recognize the previous pods, but will not automatically update them; however, you will need to use the new pod templates after manually deleting the previous pods from the nodes.

Jobs

Jobs are workloads used by Kubernetes to offer a more task-built workflow where the running containers are expected to exit successfully after completing the workload. Unlike the characteristic pod which is used to run long-running processes, jobs allow you to manage pods that are required to be terminated rather than being redeployed. A job can create one or more pods and guarantees the termination of a particular number of pods. Jobs can be used to achieve a typical batch-job such as backing up a database or deploying workers that need to function off a specific queue, i.e., image or video converters. There are various types of jobs as discussed below:

Non-parallel Jobs

In this type of job, one pod is usually initiated and goes on to complete the job after it has been terminated successfully. Incase of a failure in the pod, another one is created almost immediately to take its place.

Parallel Job with a fixed completion count

In a parallel job with a fixed completion count, a job is considered complete when there is one successful pod for every value between 1 and the number of completions specified.

Parallel Jobs with a work queue

With parallel jobs with a work queue, no pod is terminated lest the work queue is empty. This means that even if the worker performed its job, the pod could only be terminated successfully when the worker approves that all its fellow workers are also done. Consequently, all other pods are required to be terminated in the process of existing. Requested parallelism can be defined by parallel Jobs. For instance, if a job is set to 0, then the job is fundamentally paused until it is increased. It is worth noting that parallel jobs cannot support situations which require closely-communicating parallel processes, for example, in scientific computations.

CronJobs

CronJobs are used to schedule jobs or program the repetition of jobs at a specific point in time. They are analogous to jobs but with the addition of a schedule in Cron format.

ConfigMaps and Secrets

Kubernetes offers two separate storage locations for storing configuration information: Secrets for storing sensitive information and ConfigMaps for storing general configuration. Secrets and ConfigMaps are very similar in usage and support some use cases. ConfigMaps provides a mechanism of storing configuration in the environment rather than using code. It is important to store an application's configuration in the environment since an application can change configuration through development, staging, production, etc.; therefore, storing configuration in the environment increases portability of applications. ConfigMaps and Secrets are discussed below in detail.

Secrets

As mentioned above, Secrets are important for storing miniature amounts, i.e., less than I MB each of sensitive information such as keys, tokens, and passwords, etc. Kubernetes has a mechanism of creating and using Secrets automatically, for instance, Service Account token for accessing the API from a pod and it is also easy for users to create their passwords. It is quite simple to use passwords; you just have to reference them in a pod and then utilize them as either file at your own specified mount points, or as environmental variables in your pod. Note that each container in your pod is supposed to access the Secret needs to request it explicitly. However, there is no understood mechanism of sharing of Secrets inside the pod.

PullSecrets are a special type of Secret that can be used to bypass a Docker or another container image registry login to the Kubelet so that it can extract a private image for your pod. You need to be extremely cautious when updating Secrets that are in use by running pods since the pods in operation would not automatically pull the updated Secret. Additionally, you will need to explicitly update your pods, i.e., using the rolling update functionality of Deployments discussed above, or by restarting or recreating them. Put in mind that a Secret is namespaced, meaning that they are placed on a specific namespace, and only pods in the same namespace can access the Secret.

Secrets are stored in tmpfs and only stored on nodes that run pods which utilize those Secrets. The tmpfs keep Secrets from being accessible by the rest of the nodes in an application. Secrets are transmitted to and from the API server in plain text; therefore, you have to implement the SSL/TLS protected connections between user and API server and additionally between the API server and kubelets.

To enhance security for secrets, you should encrypt secrets in etcd. To add another layer of security, you should enable Node Authorization in Kubernetes, so that a kubelet can only request Secrets of Pods about its node. This function is to decrease the blast radius of a security breach on a node.

ConfigMaps

ConfigMaps are arguably similar to Secrets, only that they are designed to efficiently support working with strings that do not contain sensitive information. ConfigMaps can be used to store individual properties in the form of key-value pairs; however, the values can also be entirely used to configure files or JSON blobs to store more information. Configuration data can then be used to:

- Configure the environmental variable.

- Command-line arguments for a container.

- Configure files in a volume.

- Storing configuration files for tools like Redis or Prometheus which allows you to change the configuration of containers without having to rebuild the entire container.

ConfigMaps differs from Secrets in that it necessarily gets updated without the need to restart the pods which use them. Nevertheless, depending on how to implement the configuration provided, you may need to reload the configs, e.g., using an API call to Prometheus to reload. This is often done through a sidecar container in the same pod watching for changes in the config file.

The most important thing about ConfigMaps and Secrets is that they function to enhance the versatility of containers by limiting their specificities which allow users to deploy them in different ways. Therefore, users are provided with a choice of reusing containers or among teams, or even outside the organization due to the elimination of container specificity. Secrets are especially helpful when sharing with other teams and organizations, or even when sharing publicly. This enables you to freely share images, for instance, via a public respiratory, without having to worry about any company-specific or sensitive data being published.

How is it going till now? Before moving to the deployment part just recap the topics you just went through. Also, can you spare some time and review the book?

3. Deployments

In Kubernetes, deployments are essential for deploying and managing software; therefore, it is important to comprehend how they function and how to use effectively. Before deployment, there were Replication Controllers, which managed pods and ensured a certain number of them were operating. With deployments, we moved to ReplicaSets, which replaced Replication Controllers later on. ReplicaSets are not usually managed; rather they get managed by Deployments we define through a definite chain, i.e., Deployment-ReplicaSet-Pod(s). In addition to what ReplicaSets offer, Deployment offers you declarative control over the update strategy used for the pods. This replaces the old kubectl rolling-update way of updating, but offers similar flexibility regarding defining maxSurge and maxUnavailable, i.e., how many additional and how many unavailable pods are allowed.

Deployments can manage your updates and even go as far as checking whether or not a new version being rolled out is working, and stop the rollout in case it is not. Additionally, you can indicate a wait time needed by a pod to be ready without any of its containers crashing before it's considered available, prevents "bad updates" giving your containers plenty of time to get ready to handle traffic. Furthermore, Deployments store a history of their revisions which can be used in rollback situations, as well as an event log, that can be used to audit releases and changes to your Deployment.

Integrating Storage Solutions and Kubernetes

Today, organizations are struggling to deliver solutions which will allow them to meet quickly changing business needs, as well as to address competitive pressure. To achieve this, they are utilizing various technologies such as containers, Kubernetes, and programmable infrastructure to achieve continuous integration/continuous development (CI/CD) and DevOps transformations.

For organizations deploying these technologies, they have to ensure tenacious storage across containers as it is important to maximize the number of applications in the model. One such example of an integrated storage solution which can be integrated to Kubernetes is NetApp Trident which is discussed in detail below.

NetApp Trident

Unlike competitive application container orchestration and dynamic storage provisioning plugins, NetApp Trident integrates with Kubernetes' persistent volume (PV) framework. Red Hat OpenShift with Trident provides one interface for dynamic provision of a persistent volume of applications across storage classes. These interfaces can be allocated to any of the storage platforms

177

from NetApp to deliver the optimal storage management capabilities and performance for each application.

Trident was developed as an open source project by NetApp to offer Kubernetes users an external mechanism of monitoring Kubernetes volume and to completely automate the provisioning process. Trident can be integrated to Kubernetes and deployed as a physical server for storage, a virtual host, or a Kubernetes Pod. Trident offers Kubernetes a persistent storage solution and can be used in situations such as:

- In cloud-native applications and microservices.

- Traditional enterprise applications deployed in a hybrid cloud.

- DevOps teams who want to accelerate the CI/CD pipeline.

Trident also provides a boost of advanced features which are designed to offer deployment flexibility in

Kubernetes containerized applications, in addition to providing basic persistent volume integration. With Trident, you can:

- Configure storage via a simple Representational State Transfer application programming interface (REST API) with unique concepts that contain specific capabilities to Kubernetes storage classes.

- Protect and manage application data with NetApp enterprise-class storage. Current storage objects, such as volumes and logical unit numbers (LUNs), can easily be used by Trident.

- Based on your choice, you can use separate NetApp storage backends and deploy each with different configurations, thus allowing Trident to provide and consume storage with separate features, and present that storage to container-deployed workloads in a straightforward fashion.

Integrating the Trident dynamic storage provider to Kubernetes as a storage solution offers numerous benefits outlined below:

- Enables you to develop and deploy applications faster with rapid iterative testing.

- It provides a dynamic storage solution across storage classes of the entire storage portfolio of SolidFire, E-Series, NetApp, and ONTAP storage platforms.

- Improves efficiency when developing applications using Kubernetes.

Deploying Real World Application

To give you a better idea on how to deploy the real-world application, we are going to use a real-world application, i.e., Parse.

Parse

Parse is a cloud API designed to provide easy-to-use storage for mobile applications. It offers a variety of different client libraries making it easy to integrate with Android, iOS and other mobile platforms. Here is how you can deploy Parse in Kubernetes:

Fundamentals

Parse utilizes MongoDB cluster for its storage, therefore, you have to set up a replicated MongoDB using Kubernetes StatefulSets. Additionally, you should have a Kubernetes cluster deployed and ensure that the kubectl tool is properly configured.

Building the parse-server

The open source parse-server comes with a Dockerfile for easy containerization of the clone Parse repository.

```
$ git clone
https://github.com/ParsePlatform/pars
e-server
```

Then move into that directory and build the image:

$ cd parse-server

$ docker build -t ${DOCKER_USER}/parse-server.

Finally, push that image up to the Docker hub:

$ docker push ${DOCKER_USER}/parse-server

Deploying the parse-server

Once a container image is developed, it is easy to deploy the parse-server into your cluster using the environmental variables configuration below:

APPLICATION-ID-An identifier for authorizing your application.

MASTER-KEY-An identifier that authorizes the master user.

DATABASE-URI-It is the URI for your MongoDB cluster.

When all these are placed together, it is

possible to deploy Parse as a Kubernetes Deployment using the YAML as illustrated below:

```
apiVersion: extensions/v1beta1
kind: Deployment
metadata:
  name: parse-server
  namespace: default
spec:
  replicas: 1
  template:
    metadata:
      labels:
        run: parse-server
    spec:
      containers:
      - name: parse-server
        image: ${DOCKER_USER}/parse-server
        env:
        - name: DATABASE_URI
          value: "mongodb://mongo-0.mongo:27017,\
            mongo-1.mongo:27017,mongo-2.mongo\
            :27017/dev?replicaSet=rs0"
        - name: APP_ID
          value: my-app-id
        - name: MASTER_KEY
          value: my-master-key
```

Testing Parse

It is important to test the deployment and this can be done by exposing it as a

183

Kubernetes service as illustrated below:

```
apiVersion: v1
kind: Service
metadata:
  name: parse-server
  namespace: default
spec:
  ports:
  - port: 1337
    protocol: TCP
    targetPort: 1337
  selector:
    run: parse-server
```

After testing confirms its operation, the parse then knows to receive a request from any mobile application; however, you should always remember to secure the connection with HTTPS after deploying it.

How to Perform a Rolling Update

A rolling update refers to the process of updating an application regarding its configuration or just when it is new. Updates are important as they keep applications up and running; however, it is impossible to update all features of an application all at once since the application will likely experience a downtime. Performing a rolling update is therefore important as it allows you to catch errors during the process so that you can rollback before it affects all of your users.

Rolling updates can be achieved through the use of Kubernetes Replication Controllers and the kubectl rolling-update command; however, in the latest version, i.e., Kubernetes 1.2, the Deployment object API was released in beta. Deployments function at a more advanced level as compared to Controllers and therefore are the preferred mechanism of performing rolling updates. First, let's look at how to complete a rolling update with a replication controller then later using Deployment API.

Rolling Updates with a Replication Controller

You will need a new a new Replication Controller with the updated configuration. The rolling update process synchronizes the rise of the replica count for the new Replication Controller, while lowering the number of replicas for the previous Replication Controller. This process lasts until the desired number of pods are operating with the new configuration defined in the new Replication Controller. After the process is completed, the old replication is then deleted from the system. Below is an illustration of updating a deployed application to a newer version using Replication Controller:

```
apiVersion: v1
kind: ReplicationController
metadata:
  name: k8s-deployment-demo-controller-v2
spec:
  replicas: 4
  selector:
    app: k8s-deployment-demo
    version: v0.2
  template:
    metadata:
      labels:
        app: k8s-deployment-demo
        version: v0.2
    spec:
      containers:
        - name: k8s-deployment-demo
          image: ryane/k8s-deployment-demo:0.2
          imagePullPolicy: Always
          ports:
            - containerPort: 8081
              protocol: TCP
          env:
            - name: DEMO_ENV
              value: production
```

To perform an update, kubectl rolling-update is used to stipulate that we want to update the running k8s-deployment-demo-controller-v1 Replication controller to k8-deployment-demo-controller-v2as illustrated below:

```
$ kubectl rolling-update k8s-deployment-demo-controller-v1 --updat
```

187

Rolling updates with a Replication Controller faces some limitations, such that if you store your Kubernetes displays in source control, you may need to change at least two manifests to co-ordinate between releases. Additionally, the rolling update is more susceptible to network disruptions, coupled with the complexity of performing rollbacks, as it requires performing another rolling update back to another Replication Controller with an earlier configuration thereby lacking an audit trail. An easier method was developed to perform rolling updates with a deployment as discussed below:

Rolling Updates with a Deployment

Rolling updates with a deployment is quite simple, and similar rolling updates with Replication Control with a few differences are shown below:

```
apiVersion: extensions/v1beta1
kind: Deployment
metadata:
  name: k8s-deployment-demo-deployment
spec:
  replicas: 4
  selector:
    matchLabels:
      app: k8s-deployment-demo
  minReadySeconds: 10
  template:
    metadata:
      labels:
        app: k8s-deployment-demo
        version: v0.1
    spec:
      containers:
        - name: k8s-deployment-demo
          image: ryane/k8s-deployment-demo:0.1
          imagePullPolicy: Always
          ports:
            - containerPort: 8081
              protocol: TCP
          env:
            - name: DEMO_ENV
              value: staging
```

The differences are

- The selector uses match labels since the Deployment objects support set-based label requirements.

- The version label is excluded by the selector. The same deployment object supports multiple versions of the application.

The kubectl create function is used to run the deployment as illustrated below:

```
$ kubectl create -f demo-deployment-v1.yml --record
deployment "k8s-deployment-demo-deployment" created
```

This function saves the command together with the resource located in the Kubernetes API server. When using a deployment, four pods run the application to create the Deployment objects as shown below:

As mentioned earlier on, one advantage of using deployment is that the update history is always stored in Kubernetes and the kubectl rollout command can be

```
$ kubectl get pods
NAME                                               READY    STATU!
k8s-deployment-demo-deployment-3774590724-2scro    1/1      Runnir
k8s-deployment-demo-deployment-3774590724-cdtsh    1/1      Runnir
k8s-deployment-demo-deployment-3774590724-dokm9    1/1      Runnir
k8s-deployment-demo-deployment-3774590724-m58pe    1/1      Runnir

$ kubectl get deployment
NAME                              DESIRED   CURRENT   UP-TO-DATE
k8s-deployment-demo-deployment    4         4         4
```

used to view the update history illustrated below:

```
$ kubectl rollout history deployment k8s-deployment-demo-deployme
deployments "k8s-deployment-demo-deployment":
REVISION        CHANGE-CAUSE
1               kubectl create -f demo-deployment-v1.yml --record
2               kubectl apply -f demo-deployment-v2.yml --record
```

In conclusion, rolling updates is an essential feature in Kubernetes, and its efficiency is improved with each released version. The new Deployment feature in Kubernetes 1.2 provides a well-designed mechanism of managing application deployment.

Statefulness: Deploying Replicated Stateful Applications

Statefulness is essential in the case of the following application needs:

- Stable, persistent storage.

- Stable, unique network

191

identifiers.

- Ordered, automated rolling updates.

- Ordered, graceful deletion and termination.

- Ordered, graceful deployment and scaling.

In the above set of conditions, synonymous refers to tenacity across pod (re)scheduling.

Statefulness can be used instead of using ReplicaSet to operate and provide a stable identity for each pod. StatefulSet resources are personalized to applications where instances of the application must be treated as non-fungible individuals, with each having a stable name and state. A StatefulSet ensures that those pods are rescheduled in such a way that they maintain their identity and state. Additionally, it allows one to easily and efficiently scale the number of pets up and down. Just like ReplicaSets, StatefulSet has an anticipated replica count field which determines the number of pets you want operating at a given time. StatefulSet created pods from pod templates specific to the parts of the StatefulSet; however, unlike pods developed by ReplicaSets, pods created by the StatefulSet are not identical to each other. Each pod has its own set of volumes, i.e., storage, which differentiates it from its peers. Pet pods have a foreseeable and stable identity as opposed to new pods which gets a completely random number.

Every pod created by StatefulSet is allocated a zero index, which is then utilized to acquire the pod's name and hostname and to ascribe stable storage to the pod; therefore, the names of the pods are predictable since each pod's name is retrieved from the StatefulSet's name and the original index of the instance. The pods are well organized rather than being given random names.

In some situations, unlike regular pods, Stateful pods require to be addressable by their hostname, but this is not the case with regular pods.

Attributed to this, StatefulSet needs you to develop a corresponding governing headless service that is used to offer the actual network distinctiveness to each pod. In this service, each pod, therefore, gets its unique DNS entry; thus, its aristocracies and perhaps other clients in the network can address the pod by its hostname.

Deploying a Replicated Stateful Application

To deploy an app through StatefulSet, you will first need to create two or more separate types of objects outlined below:

- The StatefulSet itself.

- The governing service required by the StatefulSet.

- PersistentVolume for storing the data files.

The StatefulSet is programmed to develop a PersistantVolumeClaim for

194

every pod instance which will then bind to a persistent volume; however, if your cluster does not support dynamic provisioning, you will need to manually create PersistentVolume using the requirements outlined above.

To create the PersistentVolume required to scale the StatefulSet to more than tree replicas, you will first need to develop an authentic GCE Persistent Disks like the one illustrated below:

```
$ gcloud compute disks create --size=1GiB --zone=europe-west1-b pv-a
$ gcloud compute disks create --size=1GiB --zone=europe-west1-b pv-b
$ gcloud compute disks create --size=1GiB --zone=europe-west1-b pv-c
```

The GCE Persistent Storage Disk is used as the fundamental storage mechanism in Google's Kubernetes Engine.

The next step in deploying a replicated Stateful application is to create a governing service which is essential to provide the Stateful pods with a network identity. The governing service should contain:

- Name of the Service.

- The StatefulSet's governing service which should be headless.

- Pods which should be allotted labels synonymous to the service, i.e., app=kubia label.

After completing this step, you can then create the StatefulSet manifest as listed below:

```
apiVersion: apps/v1beta1
kind: StatefulSet
metadata:
  name: kubia
spec:
  serviceName: kubia
  replicas: 2
  template:
    metadata:
      labels:                          1
        app: kubia                     1
    spec:
      containers:
      - name: kubia
        image: luksa/kubia-pet
        ports:
        - name: http
          containerPort: 8080
          volumeMounts:
          - name: data                 2
            mountPath: /var/data       2
  volumeClaimTemplates:
  - metadata:                          3
      name: data                       3
    spec:                              3
      resources:                       3
        requests:                      3
          storage: 1Mi                 3
      accessModes:                     3
      - ReadWriteOnce                  3
```

Later on, create the StatefulSet and a list
of pods. The final product is that the
StatefulSet will be configured to develop
two replicas and will build a single pod.
The second pod is then created after the
first pod has started operating.

197

Understanding Kubernetes Internals

To understand Kubernetes internals, let's first discuss the two major divisions of the Kubernetes cluster:

- The Kubernetes Control Plane

- Nodes

- Add-on Components

The Kubernetes Control Panel

The control panel is responsible for overseeing the functions of the cluster. The components of the control panel include:

- The etcd distributed persistent storage

- The Controller Manager

- The Scheduler

- The API server

The components function is in unison to store and manage the state of the cluster.

Nodes

The nodes function to run the containers and have the following components:

- The Kubelet

- The Container Runtime (Docker, rkt, or others)

- The Kubernetes Service Proxy (kube-proxy)

Add-on Components

Apart from the nodes and control panel, other components are required for Kubernetes to operate effectively. This includes:

- An Ingress controller

- The Dashboard

- The Kubernetes DNS server

- Heapster

- The Container Network Interface network plugin

Functioning of the Components

All the components outlined above interdepend among each other to function effectively; however, some components can carry out some operations independently without the other components. The components only communicate with the API server and not to each other directly. The only component that communicates with the etcd is the API server. Rather than the other components communicating directly with the etcd, they amend the cluster state by interacting with the API server. The system components always initiate the integration between the API server and other components. However, when using the command kubectl to retrieve system logs, the API server does not connect to the Kubelet and you will need to use kubectlattachorkubectl port-forward to connect to an operating container.

The components of the worker nodes can be distributed across multiple servers, despite components placed on the worker nodes operating on the same node. Additionally, only a single instance of a Scheduler and Controller Manager can be active at a time in spite of multiple instances of etcd and the API server being active concurrently performing their tasks in parallel.

The Control Plane components, along with the kube-proxy, run by either being deployed on the system directly or as pods. The Kubelet operates other components, such as pods, in addition to being the only components which operate as a regular system component. The Kubelet is always deployed on the master, to operate the Control Plane components as pods.

Kubernetes using etcd

Kubernetes uses etcd which is a distributed, fast, and reliable key-value store to prevent the API servers from failing and restarting due to the operating pressure experienced by storing the other components. As previously mentioned, Kubernetes is the only system component which directly communicates to etcd, thereby has a few benefits which include enhancing the optimistic locking system coupled with validation, and providing the only storage location for storing cluster state and metadata.

Function Of The Api Server

In Kubernetes, the API server is the primary component used by another system component as well as clients such as kubectl. The API server offers a CRUD (Create, Read, Update, and Delete) interface, which is important for querying and modifying the cluster state over a RESTful API in addition to storing the state in etcd. The API server is also a validation of objects to prevent clients from storing improperly constructed objects. Additionally, it also performs optimistic locking, therefore, variations in an object are never superseded by other clients in the situation of concurrent updates.

It is important to note that the API server does not perform any other task away from what is discussed above. For instance, it does not create pods when you develop a ReplicaSet resource, nor does it overlook the endpoints of a service. Additionally, the API server is not responsible for directing controllers to perform their task; rather, it allows controllers and other system components to monitor changes to deployed resources.

kubectlis an example of an API server's client tool and is essential for supporting watching resources. For instance, when deploying a pod, you don't have to continuously poll the list of pods by repeatedly executing kubectl get pods.

Rather, you may use the watchflag to be notified of each development, modification, or deletion of a pod.

The Function of Kubelet

In summary, Kubelet is in charge of every operation on a worker node. Its main task is to register the node it is operating by creating a node resource in the API server. Also, it needs to constantly oversee the API server for pods that have been scheduled to the node, and the start of the pod's container. Additionally, it continuously monitors running containers and informs the API server of their resource consumption, status, and events.

The other functionality of Kubelet is to run the container liveness probes and restarting containers following the failure of probes, in addition to terminating containers when their pod is deleted from the API server and notifies the server that the pod has been terminated.

Securing the Kubernetes API Server

Think of this situation; you have an operational Kubernetes cluster which is functioning on a non-secure port accessible to anyone in the organization. This is extremely dangerous as data in the API server is exceptionally susceptible to breaches; therefore, you have to secure the API server to maintain data integrity. To secure the API server, you must first retrieve the server and client certificates by using a token to stipulate a service account, and then you configure the API server to find a secure port and update the Kubernetes master and node configurations. Here is a detailed explanation:

Transport Security

The API server usually presents a self-signed certificate on the user's machine in this format: $USER/. kube/config. The API server's certificate is usually contained in the root certificate which, when specified, can be used in the place of the system default root certificate. The root certificate is automatically placed in $USER/. kube/config upon creating a cluster using kube-up.sh

Authentication

The authentication step is next after a TLS is confirmed. In this step, the cluster creation script or cluster admin configure the API server to operate one or more Authenticator Modules made up of key components, including Client Certificate, Password, Bootstrap Tokens, Plain Tokens and JWT Tokens. Several authentication modules can be stated after trial and error until the perfect match succeeds. However, if the request cannot be authenticated, it is automatically rejected with HTTP status code 401. In the case of authentication, the user is provided with a specific username which can be used in subsequent steps. Authenticators vary widely with others providing usernames for group members, while others decline them altogether. Kubernetes uses usernames for access control decisions and in request logging.

Authorization

The next step is the authorization of an authenticated request from a specified user. The request should include the username of a requester, the requested action, and the object to be initiated by request. The request is only authorized by an available policy affirming that the user has been granted the approval to accomplish the requested action.

With Kubernetes authorization, the user is mandated to use common REST attributes to interact with existing organization-wide or cloud-provider-wide access control systems. Kubernetes is compatible with various multiple authorization modules such as ABAC mode, RBAC Mode, and Webhook mode.

Admission Control

This is a software module that functions to reject or modify user requests. These modules can access the object's contents which are being created or updated. They function on objects being created, deleted, updated or connected. It is possible to configure various admission controllers to each other through an order. Contrary to Authentication and Authorization Modules, the Admission Control Module can reject a request leading to the termination of the entire request. However, once a request has been accepted by all the admission controllers' modules, then it is validated via the conforming API object, and then written to the object store.

Securing Cluster Nodes and Networks

In addition to securing a Kubernetes API server, it is also extremely important to secure cluster nodes and networks as it is the first line of defense to limit and control users who can access the cluster and the actions they are allowed to perform. Securing cluster nodes and networks involves various dimensions which are listed below and are later discussed in detail:

- Controlling access to the Kubernetes API

- Controlling access to the Kubelet

- Controlling the capabilities of a workload or user at runtime

- Protecting cluster components from compromise

Controlling Access to the Kubernetes API

The central functionality of Kubernetes

lies with the API, therefore, should be the first component to be secured. Access to the Kubernetes API can be achieved through: Using Transport Level Security (TLS) for all API traffic - It a requirement by Kubernetes that all API communication should be encrypted by default with TLS, and the majority of the installation mechanism should allow the required certificates to be developed and distributed to the cluster component.

API Authentication - The user should choose the most appropriate mechanism of authentication, such that the accessed pattern used should match those used in the cluster node. Additionally, all clients must be authenticated, including those who are part of the infrastructure like nodes, proxies, the scheduler and volume plugins.

API Authorization - Authorization happens after authentication, and every request should pass an authorization check. Broad and straightforward roles may be appropriate for smaller clusters and may be necessary to separate teams into separate namespaces when more users interact with the cluster.

Controlling access to the Kubelet

Believe it or not, Kubelets allow unauthenticated access to the API server as it exposes HTTPS endpoints, thereby providing a strong control over the node and containers. However, production clusters, when used effectively, enable Kubelet to authorize and authenticate requests thus securing cluster nodes and networks

Controlling the capabilities of a workload or user at runtime

Controlling the capabilities of a workload can secure cluster nodes by ensuring high-level authorization in Kubernetes. This can be done through:

- Limiting resource usage on a cluster

- Controlling which privileges containers run with

- Restricting network access

- Restricting cloud metadata API access

- Controlling which nodes Pods may access

Protecting cluster components from compromise

By protecting cluster components from compromise, you can secure cluster nodes and networks by:

- Restricting access to etcd

- Enable audit logging

- Restricting access to alpha and beta features

- Reviewing third-party integrations before enabling them

- Encrypting secrets at rest

- Receiving security alert updates and reporting vulnerabilities

Managing Pods Computational Resources

When creating pods, it is important to consider how much CPU and computer memory a pod is likely to consume, and the maximum amount it is required to consume. This ensures that a pod is only allocated the required resources by the Kubernetes cluster, in addition to determining how they will be scheduled across the cluster. When developing pods, it is possible to indicate how much CPU and memory each container requires. After the specifications have been indicated, the scheduler then decides on how to allocate each pod to a node.

Each container of a pod can specify the required resources as shown below:

- `spec.containers[].resources.limits.cpu`

- `spec.containers[].resources.limits.memory`

- `spec.containers[].resources.requests.cpu`

- `spec.containers[].resources.requests.memory`

While computational resources requests and limits can only be specified to individual containers, it is essential to indicate pod resource and request as well. A pod resource limit stipulates the amount of resource required for each container in the pod.

When a pod is created, the Kubernetes scheduler picks a node in which the pod will operate on. Each node has a maximum limit for each of the resource type, i.e., the memory and CPU. The scheduler is tasked to ensure that the amount of each requested resource of the scheduled containers should always be less than the capacity of the node. The scheduler is highly effective that it declines to place a pod on a node if the actual CPU or memory usage is

213

extremely low and that the capacity check has failed. This is important to guard against a shortage in the resource on a node incase of an increase in resource usage later, for instance, during a period peak in the service request rate.

Running OF PODS with Resource limits

When a container of a pod is started by Kubelet, it passes the CPU and memory limits to the container runtime as a confirmatory test. In this test, if a container surpasses the set memory limit, it might be terminated. However, if it is restartable, the Kubelet will restart it, together with any form of runtime failure. In the case that a container exceeds its memory specifications, the pod will likely be evicted every time the node's available memory is exhausted. A container is not allowed to outdo its CPU limit for extended periods of time, although it will not be terminated for excessive CPU usage.

Automatic scaling of pods and cluster nodes

Pods and cluster nodes can be manually scaled, mostly in the case of expected load spikes in advance, or when the load changes gradually over a longer period, requiring manual intervention to manage a sudden, unpredictable increase in traffic or service request. Manual scaling is not efficient and it is ideal, therefore, that Kubernetes provides an automatic mechanism to monitor pods and automatically scale them up in situations of increased CPU usage attributed to an increase in traffic.

The process of autoscaling pods and cluster nodes is divided into three main steps:

- Acquiring metrics off all the pods that are managed by the scaled resource object.

- Calculating the number of pods required to maintain the metrics at the specified target value.

- Update the replicas field of the scaled resource.

The process commences with the horizontal pod autoscaler controller, obtaining the metrics of all the pods by querying Heapster through REST calls. The Heapster should be running in the cluster for autoscaling to function once the Autoscaler obtains the metrics for the pod belonging to the system component in a question of being scaled. The Autoscaler then uses the obtained metrics to determine the number that will lower the average value of the metric across all the replicas as close as possible. This is done by adding the metric values obtained from all the pods and dividing the value by the target value set on the HorizontalPodAutoscaler resource and then rounding the value to the next larger value. The final step of autoscaling is updating the anticipated replica count field on the scaled component and then allowing the

Replica-Set controller to spin up additional pods or delete the ones in excess altogether.

Extending Kubernetes Advanced Scheduling

Kubernetes has an attribute of being an advanced scheduler; therefore, it provides a variety of options to users to stipulate conditions for allocating pods to particular nodes that meet a certain condition, rather than basing it on available resources of the node. Kubernetes advanced scheduling is achieved through the master API which is a component that provides offers to read/write access to the cluster's desired and current state. The scheduler uses the master API to retrieve existing information, carry out some calculations and then update the API with new information relating to the desired state.

Kubernetes utilizes controller patterns to uphold and update the cluster state where the scheduler controller is particularly responsible for pod-scheduling decisions. The scheduler constantly monitors the Kubernetes API to find unscheduled pods and decides on which node the pods will be placed on. The decision to create a new pod by the scheduler is achieved after three stages:

- Node filtering

- Node priority calculation

- Actual scheduling operation

In the first stage, the scheduler identifies a node which is compatible with the running workload. A compatible node is identified by passing all nodes via a set of filters and eliminating those which are not compatible with the required configurations. The following filters are used:

- Volume filters

- Resource filters

- Affinity selectors

In addition to scheduling, cluster users and administrators can update the

218

cluster state by viewing it via the Kubernetes dashboard which enables them to access the API.

Best Practices for Developing Apps

After going through much of the content in developing applications with Kubernetes, here are some of the tips for creating, deploying and running applications on Kubernetes.

Building Containers

- Keep base images small - It is an important practice to start building containers from the smallest viable image and then advancing with bigger packages as you continue with the development. Smaller base images have some advantages including it builds faster, it has less storage, it is less likely to attack surface and occupies less storage.

- Don't trust just any base image -

Most people would just take a created image from DockerHub, and this is dangerous. For instance, you may be using a wrong version of the code, or the image could have a bug in it, or, even worse, it could be a malware. Always ensure that you use your base image.

Container Internals

- Always use a non-root user inside the container - A non-root user is important in the situation that someone hacks into your container and you haven't changed the user from a root. In this situation, the hacker can access the host via a simple container escape but, on changing the user to non-root, the hacker will need numerous hack attempts to gain root access.

- Ensure one process per container - It is possible to run more than one process in a container; however, it is advised to run only a single process since Kubernetes manages containers based on their health.

Deployments

- Use plenty of descriptive labels when deploying - Labels are arbitrary key-value pairs, therefore, are very powerful deployment tools.

- Use sidecars for Proxies, watchers, etc. - A group of processes may be needed to communicate with one another, but they should not run on a single container.

How to Deploy Applications That Have Pods with Persistent Dependencies

You can have applications having persistent pod dependencies using the Blue-Green Deployment mechanism. This mechanism involves operating two versions of an application concurrently, and moving production traffic between the old and new version. The Blue-Green deployment mechanism switches between two different versions of an application which support N-1 compatibility. The old and new versions of the application are used to distinguish between the two apps.

How to Handle Back-Up and Recovery Of Persistent Storage In The Context Of Kubernetes

Persistent storage in Kubernetes can be handled with etcd which is a consistent and an essential key-value store since it acts as a storage location for all Kubernetes' cluster data. They ensure the correct functioning of etcd, and the following requirements are needed:

- Check out for resource starvation

- Run etcd as a cluster of odd members

- Ensure that the etcd leader timely relays heartbeats to followers to keep the followers stable

To ensure a smooth back-up, you may operate etcd with limited resources. Persistent storage problems can be eliminated by periodically backing up the cluster data which is essential in recovering the clusters in the case of losing master nodes. The Kubernetes states any critical information, i.e., secrets are contained in the snapshot file which can be encrypted to prevent unauthorized entry. Backing up Kubernetes clusters into the etcd cluster can be accomplished in two major ways: built-in snapshot and volume snapshot.

etcd clusters can be restored from snapshots which are taken and obtained from an etcd process of the major and minor version. etcd also supports the restoration of clusters with different patch versions. A restore operation is usually employed to recover the data of a failed cluster.

In the case of failure in the majority of etcd members, the etcd cluster is considered failed and therefore

Kubernetes cannot make any changes to its current state. In this case, the user can recover the etcd cluster and potentially reconfigure the Kubernetes API server to fix the issue.

How to Deploy an Application with Geographic Redundancy in Mind

Geo-Redundant applications can be deployed using Kubernetes via a linked pair of SDN-C. This is still a new concept developed in ONAP Beijing and involves using one site as an active site and the other site acting as a warm standby, which could also be used as an active site. The operator is tasked to monitor the health of the active site by establishing failures and initiating a scripted failover. They are also responsible for updating the DNS server so that the clients would direct their messaging towards the now-active site. A PROM component, which was added later on, can automatically update the DNS server and monitor health, thereby eliminating the need of having an operator. PROM relays the status of the site health and can make informed decisions.

4. Conclusion

In conclusion, while this guide offers you a good understanding of the essential components of Kubernetes, you have to carry out practical examples to gain a deeper understanding of the concepts. This guide only explains the basic functionalities, but does delve deeper into fundamental concepts. It is important to note that Kubernetes is a sophisticated resource for creating and deploying; therefore, you need to start with the basics as you go deeper into key functionalities. We hope this guide has been key in understanding the basic concepts of Kubernetes which are still a developing concept. Thank you

** How did you like the book? Could you spare some time and review it.

Check Out My Other Books

Below you'll find some of my other popular books that are popular on Amazon and Kindle as well. Search with name and Stephen Fleming

❖ **DevOps Handbook: Introduction to DevOps and its impact on Business Ecosystem**

❖ LOVE YOURSELF – 21 Day Plan for Learning "Self-Love" To Cultivate Self-Worth, Self-Belief, Self-Confidence, Happiness

Here Is a Preview of what you'll learn...

- Understanding Self Love

- How You Benefit From Loving Yourself Unconditionally

- Learning self-love to cultivate self-worth, self-belief & self – confidence: A 21 day action plan:

228

It covers day 1 to day 21 activities and practice to be developed into daily habits

❖ **Intermittent Fasting: 7 effective fasting techniques with scientific approach to stay healthy, lose weight, slow down aging process and live longer!**

Here Is a Preview of what you'll learn...

- Intermittent Fasting Explained: what is it, historical facts.

- The Scientific Logic behind it: How it affects the metabolism
- Benefits: proven results of intermittent fasting
- 7 Techniques: which technique has what outcome
- Tips to succeed with Intermittent Fasting: The mental aspect

**I have few free coupons of audible copy for the above titles. Reach me out if interested - Valueadd2life@gmail.com